SEARCH ME

Other titles in the Great Brand Stories series

SEARCH ME

THE SURPRISING SUCCESS OF GOOGLE

NEIL TAYLOR

CYANBOOKS

Copyright © 2005 Neil Taylor

First published in Great Britain in 2005 by
Cyan Books, an imprint of

Cyan Communications Limited
119 Wardour Street
London W1F 0UW
T: +44 (0)20 7565 6120
E: sales@cyanbooks.com
www.cyanbooks.com

The right of Neil Taylor to be identified as
the author of this work has been asserted
by him in accordance with the Copyright,
Designs and Patents Act 1988.

A CIP record for this book is available
from the British Library

ISBN 1-904879-16-0

Printed and bound in Great Britain by
TJ International, Padstow, Cornwall

CONTENTS

PREFACE

If you've been away from this world for the last ten years you might find this book deeply puzzling. It's about a brand – or is it a product? – that is absolutely free to those who use it. It's about a product – or is it a brand? – that people use to search for and find information. The Internet, the new god that shapes our lives, enables this brand to be freely distributed into homes, workplaces and remote spaces all over the world.

Google cannot quite believe its luck. In another age an idea like this would never have got off the ground. It would have involved excessive amounts of time, labor, mental capacity and physical resources to achieve tasks that are now performed in split seconds. But in the mid-1990s the technology was in place, if you were bright enough to use it. And the two young men from Stanford University were extremely bright.

Their idea was Google, and Google was a search engine, which sounds deadly dull unless you're the high-tech equivalent of a trainspotter. Like all good technology Google's miraculous ease of use hides a formidable complexity of engineering. It opens up the universe through the click of a mouse. Unlike other technological miracles Google hardly ever fails or lets us down, and it always seems the most human of companions. It makes us smile and it makes our lives better, thus achieving the most elusive task of modern branding.

But how does Google do it? How did it come about and

where will it go next? The world's great libraries are signing up with Google to make their literary treasures freely available to us all – just one mind-boggling indication of future (no, current) possibilities. Whatever the world is going to be like in ten years' time, it seems certain that Google will play a leading role in taking us there.

In *Search Me* Neil Taylor goes, appropriately enough, on a search to find the essence of Google. It's a relaxed, sometimes serendipitous journey, and that is a style that Google has made familiar to us. Along the way he explores questions about the nature and the limits of branding, relevant to any modern business. So press the "I'm feeling lucky" button, dip inside and google your way through the book.

John Simmons
Series editor, *Great brand stories*

THANK YOUS

Thank you to John Simmons, editor of the *Great brand stories* series, for encouraging me to write this book, and to John and Martin Hennessey of The Writer (www.thewriter.co.uk) for all their support over the last year. Thanks too to Sherm, Emily Butcher and Ian Ginsberg for their secret squirrel research; to all the friends and brand experts who contributed their opinions; and Nick Liddell for arguing about it (and most other things) with me.

Finally, yet more thanks to Martin, Pom and Linette at Cyan Books for helping me vastly improve my prominence in the Google listings. Learning to be able to use "–Australian" when I searched "Neil Taylor" was a big help too.

INTRODUCTION

I met Google by personal introduction. I can't even remember who it was now; all I know is that *someone* in the computer room of my university told me about a search engine I'd never heard of. It had an interesting name – fun, rather than the earnest Alta Vista (which I'd been using until then), and less self-conscious than the unbridled excitement of Yahoo! and, well, Excite. The sort of thing that might get stuck in your brain. When I got to the website, it was like a cool, crisp, sunny morning in Iceland: instead of the usual visual assault of pop-ups and banners to hijack your attention, there was cool, calm, empty white space. A children's storybook logo, and a little mouth waiting to be filled.

That was how most people found Google: by word of mouth. It is *the* word of mouth success of our times. It's one of the reasons for its success, and why only seven years into its short life (in corporate terms), it's already been voted the world's best-loved brand in Interbrand's Brandchannel survey. Twice. Now, the sole point of a brand is to get people to like it. So if Google's the one we like most, then it must be the best brand there is (and that means if you only ever read one book, about one brand, this should be it). It's also a brand that has wheedled its way into our psyche to such an extent that it's spawned a verb that's made it into the dictionary. (And stayed there: not one of these fly-by-night charlatans of media slang. Come in "F Factor," "DINKY," and "bobbit:" your time is up.)

Now it has over 8 billion documents indexed, ready to be searched by the likes of you and me, up to 300 million times a day. Nearly 54 percent of all US searches happen through Google, even if they might carry someone else's name, and the average American user spends half an hour of every month there. It might mean that you end up spending more time with Google than you do talking to your mum.

So most people would agree that this young whippersnapper is a success. It's even a big success in financial terms – in both the money it makes, and the value the market puts on the company, after its much-vaunted flotation. It's a surprising success too: it's the story of how two young students became entrepreneurs, with no corporate backers, and took on the big names of the Internet world. It's the story of a company that says it's only serious about search, cultivating an irreverent, iconoclastic attitude to everything else. Cocking a snook at the way things are normally done by the men in suits. And that snook-cocking applies to branding too, by the way. They claim that they don't promote their brand, that they're much better off worrying about the product. Hmm. We'll see about that.

This book is part of a series called *Great brand stories*. So it's my job is to suss out what, if anything, the brand has had to do with Google's success, despite its developers' protests. Helping me on the way, as we amble cheerfully, curiously, dangerously close to the Internet superhighway, will be a plethora of experts: experts in branding; experts in new media; and experts in Google. And to get to the answers, we'll need to ask a number of questions. Like these.

- **What is it that we love about Google?** After all, there are plenty of other search engines that do a similar job. Why have so many of us ended up using this one?
- **Where did Google come from? How did it grow?** We'll look at the founders, their principles, and how they influence the way things get done, and how it's become such a big hit. Maybe those will give us a clue to what makes Google a great brand.
- **What are the "basic elements" of the Google brand – the things that make it recognizable – and what do they say about the company?**
- **What's the effect of those elements? What do we feel about Google?**
- **What's it like inside Google? Does that make a difference to the brand?** Most of us will never meet anyone from Google, let alone see where they work. Yet lots of people have heard of the Googleplex, their headquarters. We'll see why what goes on inside the company has become important outside.
- **Is it really a great brand, or just the brand of a great product? Is there a difference?** Google is certainly a great product, one that millions of us interact with several times a day (for free) and with which most of us seem pretty happy. So perhaps it's just the product that we love? Can we separate the brand from the product? After all, the average user doesn't have much to go on in terms of the brand – a homepage, a logo, and not much more. So what *is* the Google brand? The big brands we've got used to over the last century belong to companies that have typically sold us tangible

things – like razors, breakfast cereals and colas – in tangible places, like shops, theme parks, cinemas. Google isn't like that. It lives in the air. When it's doing its job properly we go to its site and then we get whisked away again to where we *really* want to go. So what keeps us going back?

- **Can you be a great brand without heavy marketing and advertising?** If we *do* think the brand has had anything to do with Google's success then there's a surprise in store for the marketing people. Because here again, Google is no Coca-Cola or Pepsi. It hasn't spent millions of dollars promoting itself. In fact, it tries hard to underplay the role of its brand in its success. Instead it just went about its business quietly and waited for all of us to find it. How the heck did they manage that? Most marketing directors would kill for a megabrand that they didn't have to market, especially if they could do it in less than a measly decade. They must be doing something right.

- **What will happen to Google in the future?** Google won us over as a wee pipsqueak taking on the big boys. After its initial public offering (IPO), Google's a big boy too. Will it change them? When are they going to trip up? Or who might be the ones doing the tripping?

- And finally, and perhaps most importantly, **what can other businesses learn from the surprising success of Google?**

But before we start, there are a few things that we ought to get straight.

1. This isn't a user guide to Google

There are plenty of those out there. This is a look at Google as a business and as a brand. We will look at some of the features of the product that have made it successful, but only if they tell us something more about the Google story.

However, I will tell you that in researching this book the best thing that I've learnt is what the techies call the "negative operator." If you're searching for, say, Neil Taylor, and realize that all the results you're getting are about some over-exposed Australian painter, and not in fact, the erudite writer and brand guru you were looking for, you can persuade Google to ignore the results you don't want. You just type in the minus sign, followed by "Australian" (or whatever), and it'll ignore all the results about Neil Taylor that include that word. Genius. And that really is the only tip you're getting.

2. I'm not a techie

This isn't a user guide because, frankly, I'm not bright enough at that stuff to write one. I don't know the difference between the web and the net, and I can barely get into my own bank account online, let alone hack into anyone else's. A fairly average user of Google, in other words. Probably like you. So I won't be blinding you with science.

3. This isn't a comprehensive history of Google

The Google story is a good old yarn, and we'll need to know the important bits to understand how the character of the company, and its brand, emerged. Doubtless there are tens of thousands of techie tales waiting to be told. But not here. The brand is our hero. So techies, forgive me: I've ruthlessly expunged from my report anything I think doesn't help explain or evaluate the Google brand.

4. I'm a Google fan, but I haven't been brainwashed

I got to write this book because I'm a Google fan. When I worked for a big brand consultancy, and clients asked me which was my favorite brand, I said Google – much to the chagrin of the big brand consultancy's bosses, who'd give me a reproachful look and suggest that maybe I should mention some of our own work next time. I loved its effortless cool, and its ability to maintain an air of homemade charm – despite the fact that there are scary amounts of secret planet-crunching technology lurking behind its deceptively simple shop window. Think of the old analogy of the graceful swan gliding along as its legs kick away beneath it, and just imagine big muscular legs the size of skyscrapers underneath our feathered friend instead. That's what Google's like. There aren't many brands that inspire the same kind of loyalty; love, even. So I'm going to put my love to the test. I'm going to try to work out how it got me (and millions like me, in over a hundred countries) to feel like this: was it deliberate or accidental? For good or evil? And how can I do it and make as much money as the Google founders have?

I'm a trusting soul, and an optimist by nature. So this won't be a hatchet job, but this isn't going to be a love-in, either. Google hasn't asked me to write this book because, as I've already mentioned, it *says* it doesn't promote the brand. I'm an independent writer, free to uncover the dark corporate underbelly of Google, if there's one there lurking. And after the year it's had, it's clear it can cope with a bit of criticism.

So let's start, like most of us did, by typing www.google.com, and seeing what we get.

Chapter 1 ™

What's so special?

What is it about Google? Even in the early days of the web, there were plenty of search engines around. What was it that tickled our fancy (and what has it done to warrant a book all to itself)?

I think there are two sets of answers. The first is easy. It's about the product itself: it's about opening a browser, typing in "lyrics to Irish sea shanties," or whatever (and getting results, incredibly), and how you get what you want served up. The sort of task it might have taken you a trip to the library, some careful scouring and a quick dose of asthma from the dusty old books to do before. The second set of answers is a bit harder to define. Because Google can't just be about nuts and bolts, or why would we have voted it our best-loved brand? It's not just that Google is efficient; it seems to have a personality too that we actively like. That's the bit that gets the former brand consultant in me excited. It's about a sort of residual warm glow that stays with me once I've got what I'm after, and it's the thing that seems to seduce me (and apparently millions of others) into going back next time. Let's call these two sets of answers "the practical" and "the warm and fuzzy." If Google really is a great brand, we'll probably find it lurking in the combination of these two bits – what the product's like, and how we feel about it as a result. For now let's restrict ourselves to the former. The latter comes later. Think of it as delayed gratification.

So what do we like about it?

1. We like search engines

Search engines are a pretty amazing invention. Think of all the bizarre bits of information there are in the nether regions of the net: things that I've looked up this week include the origin of the word "chav"; what on earth that funny building is round the back of my house in Kennington (the former Lambeth workhouse, since you ask); and a recipe for a traditional Lancashire potato pie. Who on earth puts these things up there? Anyway, I've found all of them in a matter of a few minutes' canny searching, even when I've spelt things wrong or my somewhat accident-prone typing finger has slipped a bit. That search engines can understand enough of what I'm trying to ask them, find the right sort of answers and deliver it to me in under a second still makes my mind boggle. Many of the original search engine brands got bored of search pretty quickly, desperately looking for other ways to make money out of us. But we didn't get bored. And we're still not (or at least, we've become dependent on it). Just think how many times you visit one in a day, or a week.

2. It's a good search engine. Very good. Maybe even the best.

For many of us, there's still a perception that Google is the one that does it best, so all our gratitude for the wonders of the Internet ends up at its door. As John Allert, chief operating officer of Interbrand in the UK, says, "As a child I was told that computers would one day know everything about everything. That they would become virtual libraries, containing trillions of pieces of information. Google is the gateway to that library. It is a modern day Dewey Decimal system on steroids." Simon Bailey of branding consultancy Enterprise IG says, "Google is the internet equivalent of the Star Trek transporter. You type in a destination and in seconds you are transported to another time and another place, safely and quickly." And Andy Hobsbawm, chairman of new media company Agency.com, says, "when you type in a search for something there is a sense of billions of pages having been scanned on your behalf. The speed and number of pages scanned is not something users can really evaluate (keying in the word 'information' on Google returns around 800 million search results in 0.13 seconds – there's never been anything like this in human history)."

But what does best really mean for us? "Best" seems in most people's minds to mean most relevant. Yes, it's fast, but how many of us can really tell the difference between getting results in 0.18 seconds and 0.52? It might be a statistical difference of 300 percent but most of us are probably busy having a sip of tea during that time anyway. So we must have become convinced early on that Google gave us the answer closest to what we were aiming for.

And that's what Google was aiming for, too. Founder Sergey Brin has said, "Google's mission is to organize the world's information, making it universally accessible and useful. Our goal was to create a very simple and easy-to-use website that offers the best search engine in the world. This is still our goal, and we plan to continue to focus our business on search technology for some time to come."[1] Well, practice makes perfect. And Google gets a lot of practice – currently around 250 million searches a day. Google started off being recommended by a small band of very knowledgeable users. Danny Sullivan, of SearchEngineWatch.com, says "there is this core techie audience, and they love what the web used to be, and they like Google because it's clean and fast."[2]

Six years on, many of us are still in awe of Google's brain-power, and the things it can do for us. Google in the UK showed me a poem that one of its users had recently sent in:

Subject: Googlicious

Hi there,

Google is the engine that helps me every day,
When searching on the web, I always find my way.
Google lets me do my favourite things in my life.
I download lots of music. It's how I met my wife.

Tiff and I've been married for very near a year,
If it weren't for Google, I would not know my dear.
Our 1st anniversary's in August and I have a small request.
You can mull it over and do what you think best,
I'd like a Google t-shirt. I'll give it to the missus,
That's a guaranteed way to ensure more of her kisses!
I'm grateful for all you do. You are the greatest engine,
Thanks to you and all you do (and thanks for your attention)
Thanks Google.

Wow. That's the sort of feedback most brands would have framed by the front door. Indeed, the Googleplex apparently has lots of letters and photos pinned up about the place that users have sent in. Yet it's not so far from the kind of experience many of us have every day with Google (although admittedly I'm still waiting for my future wife to get in touch).

It's also reliable. Glyn Britton of brand consultancy the Ingram Partnership puts Google's magic down to "something to do with the fact that between that famously sparse home page, and the famously relevant results page, there must be something so big and clever and technical that we can't even begin to comprehend it, and yet we never see it. It never breaks. You never get an error message. It just works, beautifully." (Actually, in July 2004 it was taken down for a few hours by the MyDoom virus, with only the message "Error 27" to take its place.[3]) This consistency marks it out among worldwide brands. Hayes Roth, vice president of worldwide marketing and business development at brand consultants Landor, says: "Google is a 'problem solver' brand that works in essentially the same simple way, delivering the same core brand promise, wherever and whenever it is accessed throughout the world. There are very few other product or service brands that can make that claim on that scale."

The techies among you will also know that other search engines now claim to be as quick, as reliable and as relevant as Google. But for the time being, most of us are pretty happy with our 0.18 seconds.

3. It's simple and easy to use (and looks it too)

Not only does Google get you there safely, it gets you there, well, sort of … cleanly. It's extraordinarily easy to use. The home page and results page are deceptively simple. And this is where even the experts begin to gush, frankly. Hobsbawm says, "Google doesn't promise much and delivers lots. Its basic homepage design is a visual mnemonic for this. It's quite simply the best homepage on the web."

Rob Mitchell, the very Mitchell of new media agency Mitchell-ConnerSearson tells a story lots of us recognize – indeed, you might recognize it from the Introduction. "The first time I encountered Google, it was the height of dot.com excess and all (and I mean all) search engines were piling on features to their sites that no one wanted. And then Google appeared: a blank white page with a search box. Not only that, but it found what you were looking for quickly. And I thought: aah! Finally an antidote to this madness. I and everyone I know loved Google at first sight. And people continue to love it, because it continues to stick to its guns and do what it does, extraordinarily well."

4. It's clear about what's what

Google isn't just easy to use. It's also clear about what's what. Its search results are, Google claims, unbiased; it certainly doesn't allow people to pay to promote particular pages up the rankings, like some of its competitors. Of course Google does take advertising; it's now how it makes most of its money. But it's clear that advertising is advertising. It appears marked as "sponsored links" in a separate column on the right-hand side of the search page.

In this sense Google is like a newspaper or magazine: yes, it's a business, but its "editorial" content – in Google's case, search results – isn't tainted by commercial manipulation. We can trust the results to be the most relevant answer it can find to our query, and not the one that will make it the most money.

5. It's free!

"Most fundamentally, think about the price you pay for Google. Nada, de rien, a big nothing." That's what Yannis Kavounis of brand consultancy Onesixtyfourth thinks. A crucial element in the success of Google is that it's free. Always a winner. Very few brands consistently give us anything without us having to pay for it – free newspapers or magazines, perhaps.

But being free isn't always a path to unalloyed greatness. Sometimes we associate things that are free with cheapness, disposability. As a writer, I know that give clients work for free and often they become nightmares. They don't value your work, and feel free to change it with their every whim.

Free things also tend to have been designed to appeal to as many people as possible, or worse, an "average" person, so that you end up with something inoffensive but which no one really loves. Think of the UK's biggest free newspaper, *Metro*, which is in the hands of thousands of commuters every day but is almost stultifyingly bland.

The magic of Google is that it gives us something we want, and which is personally relevant, because we only ask it things that we want to know. We get the benefit of it being free without the downside.

Interbrand's Allert sums it up. "Google delivers. The right stuff, immediately, every time. For nothing. It asks no favours, never tries to sell me things and demands no loyalty. It takes its job quite seriously, but not itself. How many other brands can claim that?" All of these points might leave us with a nice warm feeling – a product that is impressively good at its job, and doesn't cost me a penny.

But then most of that's common to lots of search engines. Yes, when Google arrived it was doing it better than anyone else. But times have changed. People have caught up. A number of other search engines will give you similar results in a similar amount of time. Why do we keep going back to Google?

Inertia will keep people loyal for a while; most of us are pretty lazy. But familiarity and inertia don't make you *love* a brand. This general feeling of apathy on the part of customers, and potential complacency on the part of the company, can quickly send a solid old brand to the dogs, as Marks & Spencer and WH Smith have found out to their cost in the UK. At the moment, people really do love Google. The surveys prove it. So what's the secret?

Marketeers will tell you this is where your brand – as opposed to what the product actually does and how it works – comes in handy. At the point at which your products are broadly similar to your competitors', a love for a brand will keep people coming back. An emotional reaction starts to influence what we probably all like to think of as rational decision making. We'll get to looking at what that emotional reaction is in detail. But to understand the face Google presents to the world, first we need to know a bit more about Google. Why is it the best search engine? How did they make it so simple? The answer is waiting for us on a university campus in 1995.

Chapter 2™

Google beginning development

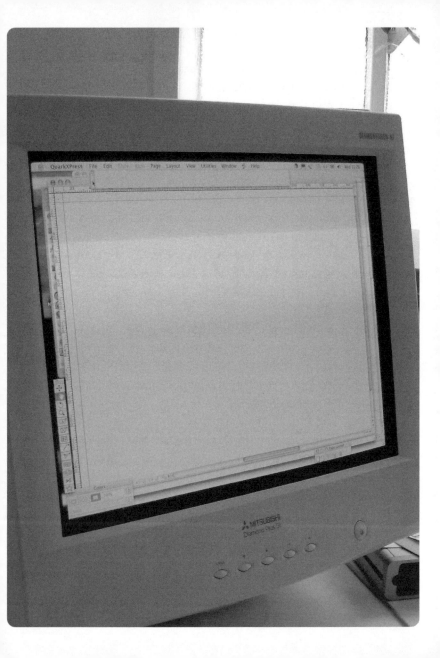

Luck or judgement? How did Google become the service we seem to love? The Google story is at the heart of Google's success. And Google is a brand that deals in stories (it's one of the reasons to be a little sceptical of their claim not to promote it). Lots of us know bits of the Google story; you might even call it the Google "mythology." Its stories became part of the brand's folklore among the audience of computer whizz-kids who were the initial champions of the brand. They in turn went round telling everyone they knew about Google until the news even trickled down to us Internet illiterates.

It's a story with two lead characters. Even if it now employs over two thousand people, to a large extent Google is two people: Larry Page and Sergey Brin. They founded the company, they're still there at the top, and their spirit seems to infuse everything that happens at Google. You could argue that they *are* the Google brand. The charismatic leader who inspires and rallies employees behind an exciting vision is something you see in the early days of many great brands. It's just unusual for that leadership to be a double act.

Page and Brin's story is a tale of hope to every computer nerd, one that starts in the USA in the late 1990s (but remember: the late 1990s was the perfect time to be an American computer nerd). They met as graduate students at Stanford University in the spring of 1995. Larry was 24, Sergey 23, and Brin was one of a number of students assigned to show Page round while he was at the university for a weekend visit. Famously they didn't hit it off. They argued. Google nearly wasn't.

Larry is the son of another computer whizz-kid, an early specialist in artificial intelligence. One of the famous Google stories is that he built an inkjet printer out of Lego, perhaps the result of being surrounded by both Lego and computer parts when he was wee. Sergey is Russian, from Moscow, but his family emigrated to the USA when he was six. It seems science is part of his DNA too: he's the son of a maths professor.

Once they got over their initial bout of mutual antipathy, they realized they did see eye to eye on computer science. They were both interested in how you could get the information you were interested in out of big amounts of data, and by the end of the year they were working together. "Data mining," as it's called, is not as easy as the likes of non-boffins like you or me might think. It's not simply a matter of picking out important words and then producing a list, although that's part of it. You also need a way to increase the probability of finding a link that's really useful. By January 1996, they were building BackRub, a proto-Google search engine which worked by analysing the "back links" that led people to websites.

If there's one thing they've got really good at over the years, it's explaining the basic principles of their brain-crushingly complex technology in language normal people might have a hope of understanding (take note, Professor Stephen Hawking). Ask Brin to explain how they harnessed the links the web needs to function, and this is the answer you get:

> It's so complex – there's not one way but many
> ways. We worked hard to understand the link

structure of the web. It's analogous to the way people provide references to one another. If I'm looking for a doctor in the area, I might go around and ask my friends to recommend good doctors. They in turn may point me to other people who know more than they do – "This guy knows the whole field of Bay Area doctors." I would then go to that person and ask him. The same thinking applies to websites. They refer to one another with links, a system that simulates referrals. The web is far more expansive and broad, however, so there must be refinements to the system. We have to look at who is doing the referring. It presents a new challenge: How do you decide the importance of the links on a site? We do it with mathematical formulas that go deeper and weigh many factors.[1]

That idea lies at the heart of what has become known as Google's PageRank™ technology. The "mathematical formulas that go deeper and weigh many factors" are the bit about which the company is notoriously secretive. Omid Kordestani, senior vice president of worldwide sales and field operations, has talked about it as Google's "special sauce."[2] The message Google don't want you to hear is that these days it's debatable just how special that special sauce really is, given that other search engines now turn up almost identical results in identical times.

Even in its infancy, this technology also reflected a principle that has become quite prominent in the subsequent Google rhetoric. That is, that it's a "democratic" way of searching the net. Google has talked about the principle like this:

> Google interprets a link from Page A to page B as a vote by Page A for Page B. But Google looks at more than the sheer volume of votes, or links, that a page receives: it also analyzes the page that casts the vote. Votes cast by pages that are themselves "important" weigh more heavily and help to make other pages "important." It is a uniquely democratic method.[3]

Perhaps more of a meritocracy than a democracy then? It's a philosophy which is now expounded (somewhat less clearly) as one of the principles of business on the Google website. It's number four in a series of "ten things" – a set of beliefs that defines the Google way of doing things. Naturally, it's a list we'll come to know pretty well over the next few chapters.

4. Democracy on the web works

Google works because it relies on the millions of individuals posting websites to determine which other sites offer content of value. Instead of relying on a group of editors or solely on the frequency with which certain terms appear, Google ranks every webpage using a breakthrough technique called PageRank™. PageRank evaluates all of the sites linking to a webpage and assigns them a value, based in part on the sites linking to them. By analyzing the full structure of the web, Google is able to determine which sites have been "voted" the best sources of information by those most interested in the information they offer. This technique actually improves as the web gets bigger, as each new site is another point of information and another vote to be counted.[4]

The early technology wasn't just unconventional in terms of the method it used. It also broke the mold in the hardware you needed to be able to do it. Conventional wisdom at the time held that you needed hefty, powerful servers to be able to do large-scale searches effectively. But you'll remember that our future heroes are lowly graduate students without big wads of cash to back them up. So instead of using big expensive machines, they wrote their own webserver, and Page found a way of using a group of much less powerful PCs to do the work. Now it's been proved this method can be quicker and more effective, and it's still at the heart of the Google approach. At the time, though, this was groundbreaking, and news of the progress the pair were making started to do the rounds.

It soon became apparent that the two had a potential business. But they later claimed to despise the mood of the day, with the dot.com bubble getting bigger by the second. Page has said, "The dot.com period was difficult for us. We were dismayed in that climate. We knew a lot of things people were doing weren't sustainable, and that made it hard for us to operate. We couldn't get good people for reasonable prices. We couldn't get office space. It was a hypercompetitive time."[5]

Instead, they bought cheap computers and ran them out of Larry's dorm room, while Sergey tried to find business partners. Ideally a nice big corporation to smooth the way for them, you'd have thought. But their refusal to hype the project, and their determination to get on with the job quietly rather than spend money "building a brand" (their own words) didn't do them any favors. Getting backing was tough going.

So in the second half of 1997 they put their PhDs "on hold" and decided to concentrate on raising some cash to build their business their way. And you can probably guess the script. In the way of these things, someone appeared who saw what our boys could do, and wanted to give them their chance. Andy Bechtolsheim was one of the founders of Sun Microsystems, and a friend of a faculty member at Stanford. He saw an early version of the technology they were now calling Google, a name based on the word "googol"

– the name for the number 10 to the power of a hundred, which you'd write as 1 followed by a hundred zeroes. And he saw potential, too. According to Sergey Brin, "We met him very early one morning on the porch of a Stanford faculty member's home in Palo Alto. We gave him a quick demo. He had to run off somewhere, so he said, 'Instead of us discussing all the details, why don't I just write you a check?' It was made out to Google Inc. and was for $100,000."[6]

One small problem was that at this point, the company Google Inc. still didn't exist. So on September 7, 1998, Google was incorporated. By the time they finished raising money, Brin and Page had nearly $1,000,000 with which to move into their first office – a garage in Menlo Park, California – and hire their first employee: Craig Silverstein, a fellow Stanford student and now Google's director of technology.

While this was happening, they were testing the commercial application of their technology through the Google.com website, and its effectiveness was beginning to get noticed, by both the trade media and the wider world. In fact, there was an audience of clued-up journalists who became strong advocates for Google, because they found it so useful themselves. It's not surprising they ended up writing about it. They raved about how good it was, its simplicity, and trademark Google quirks like the "I'm feeling lucky" button, which is still on the home page, and lets users take a punt on getting just one result to their search, hoping it's the right one.

Quickly Google found itself handling up to 10,000 search queries per day and, even this early, *PC Magazine* said that

Google was one of the Top 100 Websites and Search Engines. A ball was rolling. In six months there were another six employees, another new office, and the small matter of the number of searches going up by 500 percent.

At this point, they thought their main source of revenue would be licensing their technology for other people to use on their own sites, and that's how they got their first commercial customer. They also got another injection of cash. This time, though, it was a whopping $25,000,000 from two big venture capitalists in Silicon Valley – Sequoia Capital and Kleiner Perkins Caufield & Byers. These two were not normally bedfellows, but both took seats on the board of Google (and subsequently not surprisingly have been key in Google's move from being a private company to a public one). Soon more big companies decided to take a bet on the burgeoning Google brand: AOL/ Netscape started to use Google as the search engine for its Netcenter portal.

In 1999 Google moved again, to its current home – the famous Googleplex in Mountain View, California. Like the name Google itself, it's a play on googolplex, another number, this time ten to the power of a googol. It would take more than the rest of the book to write it down, so we'd best not dwell on thinking about that. The Googleplex, as we'll see later, is a crucial expression of what was fast becoming the unmistakable Google spirit of youth, fun, and a healthily balanced approach to work, a spirit which is pretty important to the success of the company.

By this time they were up to 3,000,000 searches a day, so by September it became clear that Google had to officially come out of "test" phase and admit it was a grown-up. As John Naughton said in the *Observer*, "For most of us Internet chronology divides into two periods – BG (Before Google) and AG. Nobody who used Google ever went back to anything else. At a click, all the other search engines were dumped on the rubbish heap of history."[7]

2000 was the year that Google really started to take the world by storm. It won Best Search Engine on the Internet, and launched 10 non-English versions of the site. In June 2000, Google officially became the search engine searching the highest number of webpages – a measly billion at that point. And on June 26, Yahoo! – then, as now, one of the biggest brands on the Internet – decided to use Google to provide search results. The endorsement of such a big brand was a big boost for Google's credibility. The small matter of 18 million searches every day was the result, and by the end of the year it was up to 60 million.

2000 was also the year that the company launched AdWords, the advertising programme that changed Google's business model and has since made it such a darling of Wall Street. After all, that's now where it gets most of its money. These were ads in a special devoted bar on the side of the page, which related to the content you'd searched for. Soon Google were claiming that advertising through Google, because it was so relevant to what users were looking for, ended up four to five times more effective than traditional web adverts.

In 2001 Google recruited Dr Eric Schmidt from Novell, as chief executive. The dynamic duo at the top had become – in their own words – a "triumvirate," and that is how it remains today. Brought in as an experienced hand at the tiller, to counterbalance the relatively green Brin and Page, Schmidt's job was to manage the company's rapid expansion, while Brin and Page kept their eye on the technological development and culture of Google. Importantly though, Eric Schmidt's PhD is in computer science, so despite his big-business CV, he can cut it with the geeks as well as the suits.

And that year, the global phenomenon truly became a global brand, launching country-specific versions of the website in the UK, Germany, France, Italy, Switzerland, Canada, Japan, and Korea, with the Google site available in 40 languages other than English, as well as an ability to search 250 million images (although admittedly Google only finds them by looking at the words associated with them). By the way, at this point we're up to an index of 3 billion web documents and 100 million searches a day.

The end of 2001 was also important in another crucial way. Two years after it was incorporated, little old Google, the upstart from Mountain View, moved into the black. It was an early signal that Google wasn't your typical dot.com. It left the ranks of the has-beens, the almost-weres and never-had-a-hope-in-hells, and joined the world of the big boys. And already the markets were eyeing it up.

From here on, it seemed to develop almost exponentially: indexing more pages, getting more searches, launching more country-specific sites and services, attracting more advertisers, being picked by more people to provide search, making more money, and adding new features: Google News, collating news stories from around the web; Google Labs, to test out new ideas; Froogle, a price comparison site; and AdWords got an overhaul which made it as cost-effective for small organizations as for big companies. In 2003 Google bought the company that produces Blogger – pioneer in the new net phenomenon of web diaries. And importantly for us, it won Interbrand's Brand of the Year for the first time, knocking Apple – another very human technology brand – off the top spot. To top it all off, it launched AdSense, which lets website owners put a bar of relevant ads in a Google-style box at the right-hand side of their own website (and split the profits between the website and Google).

2004 brought another Brand of the Year award, tests for personalized search, and the controversial Gmail e-mail. With Gmail, Google promised users masses more virtual room to store e-mails, even to the point where you'll never have to delete any. In return it uses its ad technology to scan the contents of your messages and introduce a bar of ads it thinks might be relevant. It caused an outcry, with suggestions that the scanning of personal e-mails was an invasion of personal privacy with Big Brotherish overtones. It was also the first strong hint that the Google honeymoon was over. It was now mainstream, and ripe for criticism. The backlash continued when Google announced it was selling shares in the company, and how it was planning to do it, of which more below.

Oh – Page and Brin have yet to collect their degrees.

Google now

The success of Google has been phenomenal. Today it indexes over 8,000,000,000 webpages, ready to be trawled for information when we're looking for it. It has versions of its website operating all over the world, and in many different languages. (Norway is a recent addition; it seems to have taken a long time for Google – and their lawyers – to get over the oddness of the name in the Norwegian market, where Google means "sunglasses.")

Not surprisingly, others have seen Google's stellar perform-ance – in terms of users and revenues – and are kicking them-selves that they didn't do the job. Microsoft founder Bill Gates has said, "Google kicked our butts."[8] Don't worry, he's out to remedy the situation.

But Google hasn't just made an impression in terms of sheer numbers. It's had a marked influence on our culture. There are some fairly astonishing stories of the impact Google's all-pervasiveness is having on the world. Sergey himself tells this story:

> People look up information in a life-threatening situation. Someone wrote that he was having chest pains and wasn't sure of the cause. He did a Google search, decided he was having a heart attack and called the hospital. He survived and wrote to us. To help in situations like that, Google has to be quick and correct. Other people have written us with similar stories. We get

postcards and pictures of them with their family. Those are extremes, but there are countless other examples. People are helped with their careers. Students are helped when they study. It's a powerful tool.

In October 2004, BBC News online published this report:

Google "saved" Australian hostage
An Australian journalist kidnapped in Iraq was freed after his captors checked the popular Internet search engine Google to confirm his identity.

John Martinkus was working for Australia's SBS Television

John Martinkus was seized in Baghdad on Saturday, the first Australian held hostage in Iraq since the US-led invasion.

But his captors agreed to release him after they were convinced he was not working for the CIA or a US contractor.

He was reported to be making his way home to Australia on Tuesday.

His executive producer at Australia's SBS network, Mike Carey, said Google probably saved freelance journalist Martinkus.

"They Googled him and then went onto a web site – either his own or his book publisher's web site, I don't know which one – and saw that he was who he was, and that was instrumental in letting him go, I think, or swinging their decision," he told AP news agency.[9]

As I write this book, there's an attempt going on to impeach British prime minister Tony Blair over claims he misled the Houses of Parliament on the evidence for weapons of mass destruction in Iraq. The MP behind it, Adam Price, of Welsh nationalist party Plaid Cymru, claims he was inspired to do it by an article he read online. "I was just Googling and I found it," he says.[10] If Blair falls because of Google, it will really have arrived. It shows Google is transforming our lives – through easy access to information and ideas – as few brands ever have. These are astonishing stories for a brand. In this context, it seems no wonder that we love it. It's acting like a public information service, for almost the entire world. The idea of Google as a public service is another one we'll come back to.

What is Google?

Along the way Google has grown. We still think of it as a search engine first and foremost, and indeed it is. But over the years it's added features to the main search function, and other services that complement it. Google believes these services are natural extensions to the core idea: "These are just other technologies to help you use the web. They're an alternative, hopefully a good one. But we continue to point users to the best websites and try to do whatever is in their best interest."[11]

Or, in the words of Jakob Nielsen, an industry consultant and member of Google's technical advisory council, "they operate by trying lots of things and some of them don't really work."[12] There are plenty that do, though, including:

- **Calculator:** type a sum into the search box and Google will give you the answer. It will, naturally, also give you the answer to "life, the universe + everything."
- **Froogle:** a price comparison site. Type in an item you want to buy, and Google will find the cheapest online deal.
- **Alerts:** e-mails to tell you that Google has found new information on one of your chosen searches.
- **Answers:** instead of trawling through search results, pay one of Google's researchers to give you the answer.
- **Images:** not surprisingly, this is Google's search for images. But because it finds them through words, it's not always that accurate. They don't seem to mind. Craig Silverstein, Google's director of technology, says, "If you were to type in a proverb,

and see which images pop up, then I'd expect the results to be pretty random. You can get some entertainment value out of that, and that's fine. We're happy to have Google function as an entertainment vehicle and social vehicle as well as an information vehicle."[13]

Rest assured, they'll be working on improving it.

- **News:** tracks the latest news stories from different sources across the web.
- **Definitions:** yep, Google's a dictionary too. Just type "define:" before the word you want to know.
- **AdSense:** ads targeted to the content of a webpage. Any website that uses the technology gets a share of the revenue.
- **AdWords:** the way Google helps advertisers create ads to match the keywords that people are searching for.
- **Translation:** translates foreign language sites into very bad, often incomprehensible English. (OK, maybe that isn't really fair. Translating languages is a notoriously difficult job for people, let alone computers. Google's function does at least allow you to get a vague sense of what a foreign language site might be about.)
- **The Google shop:** another let-down. The usual corporate umbrellas and bags. Symon Sweet, brand strategist at brand and design agency Bluestone, says "The Google store has the most uninspiring products you are ever likely to encounter." It's a disappointment because so much about Google is fun and unusual. So here's a tip for the triumvirate at the top: get rid of it; it's not doing you any good.

And then, of course, there are some of the companies that Google has bought to add to the list of services that it offers itself:

- **Blogger.** Devoted to helping people publish their thoughts online, get feedback, and interact with others interested in the same things. (Blogger was started by three friends at the height of the dot.com boom before Google bought it. Sound familiar?)
- **Picasa.** Designers of software that lets you organize your own library of photos and images. Now presented as "Google's Picasa."
- **Keyhole.** A 3D mapmaker, which it says will let "users view 3D images of any place on earth as well as tap a rich database of roads, businesses and many other points of interest." It is now described as "Keyhole from Google."

The consequences

Google's surprising success has had some surprising consequences. One Google-inspired phenomenon is Google bombing. Google bombing is a way of manipulating the PageRank™ system to make sure that when people type in a particular search, they see the page you want them to see. (In basic terms, this is done by getting lots of sites to link to another "target" site, using the words of the search you want to manipulate.) Of course you could use this for commercial ends, and plenty of people try. Indeed, there are even people called "optimizers," who'll advise you how to beat the Google system, and fly up the rankings, in return for a healthy fee.

Google has a big team of people trying to outwit the people who are trying to outwit Google. But more interesting are the Google bombs that aren't trying to make money, but instead want to make a political point, or make us laugh, or both at the same time. It shows that people have started to recognize the potential of Google as one of the world's primary sources of information. The most famous example of a Google bomb comes from the height of the debate over weapons of mass destruction. Type "WMD" into the search box, hit the "I'm feeling lucky" button, and the result was a parody of a typical "error" page (see overleaf).

Another threw up spoof results for the search "French military victories":

Did you mean: french military **defeats**

No standard web pages containing all your search terms were found.

Your search – **french military victories** – did not match any documents.

Suggestions:

    – Make sure all words are spelled correctly.
    – Try different keywords.
    – Try more general keywords.
    – Try fewer keywords.

Also, you can try Google Answers for expert help with your search.[14]

These Weapons of Mass Destruction cannot be displayed

The weapons you are looking for are currently unavailable. The country might be experiencing technical difficulties, or you may need to adjust your weapons inspectors mandate.

Please try the following:

- Click the [🔄] Regime change button, or try again later
- If you are George Bush and typed the country's name in the address bar, make sure that it is spelled correctly. (IRAQ).
- To check your weapons inspector settings, click the **UN** menu, and then click **Weapons Inspector Options**.
  On the **Security Council** tab, click **Consensus**. The settings should match those provided by your government or NATO.
- If the Security Council has enabled it, The United States of America can examine your country and automatically discover Weapons of Mass Destruction. If you would like to use the CIA to try and discover them, click 🔍 Detect weapons
- Some countries require 128 thousand troops to liberate them. Click the **Panic** menu and then click **About US foreign policy** to determine what regime they will install.
- If you are an Old European Country trying to protect your interests, make sure your options are left wide open as long as possible. Click the **Tools** menu, and then click on **League of Nations**. On the Advanced tab, scroll to the Head in the Sand section and check settings for your exports to Iraq.
- Click the 💣Bomb button if you are Donald Rumsfeld.[15]

Brin and Page take Google bombing in their stride. (In fact, that the WMD story remained so easy to find for so long suggests that someone at Google was in no great hurry to remove the link, as it has in other, stickier situations.) Brin says, "Typically Google bombs don't affect people looking for information." Page adds, "they're more like entertainment."

Another surprising consequence of Google's success has been the virtual annihilation of the market in buying, selling, and creating domain names. A big feature of the Internet boom in the late 1990s was the fact that anyone quick off the mark and hoping to make a quick buck or two could buy up "domain names" (words followed by .com, .net, .co.uk, or whatever) on the Internet incredibly cheaply. Not surprisingly people got in fast, buying up "generic" names like drugs.com or hotels.com, as well as those of plenty of well-known brands. This was a problem, because domain names didn't work like trademark law. In the world of trademarks, products in different categories with the same name are allowed to coexist: think of Polo mints, the VW Polo, and Polo Ralph Lauren. This works on the basis that an average customer is not likely to confuse these products – you're not likely to go into a newsagent looking for something to sweeten your breath and walk out with a small hatchback. But on the net, there is only one polo.com, so whoever got there first owned the most obvious domain name – and in the early days, that wasn't even necessarily the people who owned the brands. (Eventually the intellectual property laws were straightened out to give trademark owners effective first refusal on their own names.) Nevertheless, pretty soon most real words were taken as domain names, and the ones that weren't – you wouldn't really want to do business under those, to be honest.

The demand for domain names had two ramifications. Either other companies spent megabucks to get hold of these real-world domain names, sending a whole generation of cheeky, early-registering Internet pups into wealthy early retirement; or companies had to pay brand consultants like me to make up new words for their businesses that were not already taken as dot.coms. This climate was a significant factor in the explosion of names like Accenture, Altria, and Consignia, which the press, particularly in the UK, found ridiculous and offensive, typically characterizing them as extravagant wastes of money. It's ironic of course that these days we can't name many of the "generic" brands. Even in the net world order, brands that build a reputation and emotional resonance for their customers still seem to be more appealing than bland, generic ones. I suppose that's why the high street is full of shops bearing people's names rather than big signs saying "food" or "clothes."

Google's success was a big factor in killing that market dead (along with the disappearance of many of the Internet speculators when times got hard). People realized they could rely on Google to find the websites they were after, even if they didn't know the domain name. They started typing "BBC" into Google before they attempted bbc.com, bbc.net, bbc.co.uk or wherever else they might guess they'd find the website they were looking for, because they felt that Google was usually the easiest way to do it. Suddenly the pressure was off companies to always find the most easily guessable website, and instead people concentrated on finding ways of getting the coveted "I'm feeling lucky" slot in their chosen area. A market disappeared. And my brand-naming heyday was dead and buried.

The IPO

The big bang of Google's recent history was the selling of shares in the company. It's something that had been on the cards ever since it first broke into the black. The early board claimed they talked about floating every now and again at meetings, but never really saw the need. But it's a safe bet that some of the initial investors were eager to see a return on the money they'd put into the fledgling business.

When they finally decided to bite the bullet and float on the stock market, they did it in typical Google fashion, with little care for the traditions and conventions of Wall Street. Indeed, Sergey and Larry's letter to potential investors began with the words, "Google is not a conventional company. We do not intend to become one."[16]

What made the Google IPO different was that it was designed to maintain as much of the structure of the business as a private company as it could. The triumvirate at the top felt that was what had made it successful, so they made it clear that they would be deliberately eschewing many of the activities normally expected of a publicly quoted company. They would not be making short-term forecasts, claiming their business was too unpredictable. That way they also wouldn't be under pressure to manipulate their quarterly, half-yearly or annual results to tally with the market's expectations. They promised to keep taking risks by investing time and money in projects that were not certain to succeed, but promised great benefits on the off-chance that they did. It remains to be seen whether they can stay true to their instincts. But the two most contentious aspects of the float were the way the shares were sold, as well as the voting power those shares bought you as a Google investor.

Google chose a "Dutch auction" process to set the price of the shares, a technique rarely used in the USA. In a Dutch auction investors name the price they are willing to pay for shares, as well as the number they are willing to buy. By ranking the value of bids, and the number of shares to be taken, you can work out the highest price at which all the shares would be sold (which might, of course, be substantially less than the highest bid for shares). Google claims it chose this method so that shares would be sold at a reasonable, sustainable price, since the sale price would be a good reflection of the price the market was willing to pay. That way, it hoped to avoid the dramatic surges and falls often associated with the opening days of trading in new shares. In practice, Google modified the process, saying it could sell shares at a lower price to get a wider distribution of share ownership. This was another typically Google move – increasing the theoretical democracy of the float by making it more accessible to smaller investors, while also shielding themselves from the pressure of too many institutional investors knocking down their door for exactly the forecasts they didn't want to have to deliver.

Not surprisingly, the unconventional approach from the unconventional company got the backs up of many seasoned market-watchers. They were further aggravated by the voting structure of the company, with the shares of those at the top – the triumvirate again – having substantially more voting power than ordinary investors. To all intents and purposes this was to allow the Google Three to continue to run the business as they had as a private company. Not surprisingly then, Institutional Shareholder Services – which advises pension funds how to vote at AGMs – gives Google 0.2 out of 100 for the effectiveness of its corporate governance structure.[17] James Huguet of Great Companies said, "I just think the depth of management is not there. It's a significant challenge to build the company over a long period of time. I think there are real issues from an internal management standpoint. The company faces significant competition. We own eBay and Yahoo! and they're very well-run companies. I don't see the same quality of management with Google."[18]

In the short term though, Google's treading of the fine line between confidence and arrogance seems to be paying off, with share price steadily rising in the months since the IPO. So what is it going to do with the cash? It was something it was vague on before the float, and it remains just as vague today: "We currently have no specific plans."[19] But it's been buying, as we've seen. The 3D mapmaker Keyhole was the first big purchase after the IPO.

Some of have argued that the Google IPO spells bad news for the big banks that advise companies thinking of floating. Google didn't need the advisers to set the price for it, it got the market to do it (and do it pretty well). Google also didn't need the advisers to cozy up to the big corporate investors. It got them all

Google share price

anyway, and lots of small investors to boot. Maybe these big banks are just a waste of money?

But there are very few Googles in the world. Arguably it's only because Google is famous, and because of the enormous amount of PR and media hype it attracts, that it could do it in its own way. Because nearly all of us know Google, and lots of us like it, there was lots of interest in the IPO. In fact, quite a lot of us wanted our own little piece of it (in which case, bad luck if you live outside the USA), as much out of pride or curiosity, it seems, as the potential for any significant financial gain. It's unlikely that a less high-profile company could have kept people's attention long enough to sustain the auction. Bad news for any little company hoping to do a Google, good news for Wall Street.

In the period after the float, Google has had a run of great results, with its rate of growth recently doubling between one quarter and the next, and its share price doing the same. True to its word, Google quickly got to damping down speculation that that rate of growth would be sustainable.

Shares have recently taken a wee dip after employees and early investors sold theirs, at the end of the first of a series of "lock-ups" which will slowly ease more shares onto the open market. It means lots of Google employees could become millionaires, and will continue to line the pockets of Page and Brin, who stand to make US$1 billion by selling off some of their shares in the company. Even after that, though, they'll still own 27 percent. It looks like it'll be theirs for many years to come.

Chapter 3 ™

Google basic brand elements

So what is it that makes Google recognizably Google? What are the bits you'd go and copy if only those pesky lawyers wouldn't sue you to within an inch of your life?

If you go off to a big brand consultancy (you might remember, I used to work for one), and ask them for a new brand, or to bring your dodgy old-fashioned-looking one up to date, you usually end up with a toolkit. What a fantastic waste of £200,000, you might say. But luckily this toolkit doesn't contain wearisome practical tools like hammers and screwdrivers: instead it has all the metaphorical bits and bobs you need to keep your spanking new brand smart and shiny. Often they're called a brand's basic elements. And the Google brand has them too.

Typically, this means a logo of some kind. A set of colors (usually called a color palette, in a terribly walking-round-a-DIY-superstore-on-a-Sunday-morning kind of way). Plus a typeface which may or may not be unique to you. Some kind of visual "system" – the way you use lines, space, and so on.

And then things start to get a wee bit harder to pin down. These days brands don't just have this kind of practical stuff, they have lots of more emotional stuff too. This is where the marketing jargon gets particularly (and sometimes deliberately) woolly. You get a brand "idea," or "essence," or "positioning" – in other words, some way of expressing what the brand's about, and what makes it different from its competitors. Sometimes this is broken down into other bits too, like a vision (the brand's point of view on the world), a mission (how it's going to achieve its vision) and often a set of values – usually adjectives that describe the brand's "personality" or behavior. If you're particularly unlucky, all this information might get codified into an elegant but ultimately almost entirely baffling diagram, called something like a "brand wheel," or worse, filled in according to a template or "brand key." Then you might also get a tone of voice (I have a vested interest in making this bit sound clever and valuable, as it's what I do). Tone of voice is a way of translating the brand's values into a way of writing or speaking. So if, like Orange, you want to sound "friendly," then your tone of voice would advise you to talk about "you" and "me" rather than "our customers" and "the Company," or say things like "we'll," "isn't," and "it's," because they sound less formal than the full versions. When you start to think about the pretty massive toolkit most brands end up with, Google starts to look very simple. Let's have a look at the bits Google has.

The logo

The Google logo is a nothing more than the letters of its name, but there's a lot of personality crammed into those few letters. It's a typeface with serifs – the little sticky-out bits on the corners of traditional-style letters. But it doesn't look too old-fangled; it's not a serious buttoned-down font like Times New Roman. It's mainly lower case, and designers will tell you that that makes for a friendlier feel; AFTER ALL THINGS LOOK VERY OFFICIAL OR MAYBE VERY ANGRY IN CAPITALS. There are quirky little features, like that jaunty angle of the crossbar on the "e," and the fact that it doesn't quite reach the big bulge of the letter. Details like that make the Google letters feel slightly unusual, maybe even handmade.

There's more than a hint of the storybook about the logo: the primary colors on the big white background, the slight shadow, and the 3D quality to the letters almost sets them up to be characters in every sense of the word.

According to Google's Cindy McCaffrey, Sergey Brin designed the logo "to reflect whimsy and fun. With its colorful rounded edges, it's approachable and friendly but it's also serious about what it does."[1] It's not childish, but the logo has a charm that subliminally takes most of us back to our childhood. Of course, all of this is deliberate. It reinforces the idea that Google is simpler than the rest, and maybe even a little more innocent.

Perhaps the most famous thing about the Google logo is that it changes. Every now and again, particularly for holidays and big events, the logo gets customized with very homemade-looking cartoons. In the words of one of my more cynical sources, from a digital branding agency, who didn't want to be named:

> The logos are designed by someone who still describes himself as their "webmaster" and calls them his "doodles," [they're] not by a branding agency. Whether you choose to call their logo a "brand" is up to you; I'd just call it a logo – the kind of logo that, much like the Yahoo logo!, would come across as cheesy and a bit crap if you presented it to a client today.

Now this sort of schoolboy fun goes against one of the big rules of branding. In my brand consultant days, I repeated the mantra "keep your logo consistent" until I was blue in the face. Think of Nike, where pretty much the only brand guideline is, "don't mess with the swoosh." Look what happened to British Airways when it replaced its union flag tailfins with a series of world images; it's since gone back to the same design on every plane, thanks in no small part to one irate Margaret Thatcher, with her handy handkerchief to cover up one of the "monstrosities," and an outraged campaign from some of the more reactionary British media.

Oh well, back to Google. It's not just the "holiday logos" that change. When you do a search on Google, at the bottom of the results page, you get a little indicator as to how many pages of results it's found: "Gooogle" for just a few, "Gooooooogle" for lots and lots. You see the same playful lengthening of the name in the ads that Google provides on other people's sites. In that case, ads appear in a Google-style bar on the right-hand side of the webpage, but not in the Google logo or colors (presumably, so as not to try to "compete" with the branding of the rest of the page). But playing around with the name – even in plain text – gives you a sense of the Google personality coming through, even in that very constrained environment.

The fact that Google is willing to play around with its logo is a great way of sending a big signal that it has a sense of humor, and doesn't take itself too seriously. Not surprisingly, the holiday logos have created a minor Internet cult dedicated to spotting and collecting them. (It reminds me of the UK's Innocent drinks brand, which has a constantly changing set of stories on the side of its bottles.) There's a sense of irreverence, even iconoclasm. It's a light-hearted way of reinforcing the "anti-corporate" feel: you wouldn't get IBM playing around with its sacred blue lines.

You see this prankiness elsewhere in Google. One April Fool's Day its website replaced its usual spiel on PageRank™, and instead told us all about PigeonRank (riddled, as the more computer-literate amongst you will spot, with techie in-jokes) (see pages 62–3).

This willingness to play is one of the most important facets of Google as a brand. It shows that it wants to engage its users, and share some fun with them. And to engage someone, you need to show a little of your own humanity. A faceless corporation would not see the benefit of joking around, but a group of people would. So without having to "meet the team" in a clunky, self-conscious way, we start to feel that Google is a service run by real people with real personalities. And that's good news for me as a user, because hey, I'm a real person with a real personality too. It makes me think they're more likely to understand what I want and need from them.

The name

Now, I could go on a bit here. As I said, incredibly, I used to get paid to do nothing else but think of names for products and companies. It means I can talk about it for far too long, so if you find yourself dozing off during the next couple of paragraphs, just jump ahead to the next section.

When I was a professional namer, Google was my favorite brand name, and it still is. It's a bit of genius. Most people hate made-up names when they first hear them, and most are rightly viewed with suspicion – the Altrias and Consignias have a lot to answer for. What's so clever about Google is that although it's made up, it doesn't feel alien. It's a word that could have existed in English; it just happened not to (although now it's got the dictionary seal of approval). It's also another aspect of the Google brand that echoes childhood innocence: that "oo" sound is one that turns up in lots of other, slightly unusual, slightly fun words – oodle, caboodle, goon. And the repetition of the "g" sound adds another bit of phonetic fun and makes it even more memorable.

As we've heard, the name is supposedly based on a number. Here's what the company says about its name:

> Google is a play on the word googol, which was coined by Milton Sirotta, nephew of American mathematician Edward Kasner, and was popular-ized in the book, *Mathematics and the Imagination* by Kasner and James Newman. It refers to the number represented by the numeral 1 followed by 100 zeros. Google's use of the term reflects the company's mission to organize the immense, seemingly infinite amount of information available on the web.[3]

The technology behind Google's great results

As a Google user, you're familiar with the speed and accuracy of a Google search. How exactly does Google manage to find the right results for every query as quickly as it does? The heart of Google's search technology is PigeonRank™, a system for ranking web pages developed by Google founders Larry Page and Sergey Brin at Stanford University.

Building upon the breakthrough work of B. F. Skinner, Page and Brin reasoned that low cost pigeon clusters (PCs) could be used to compute the relative value of web pages faster than human editors or machine-based algorithms. And while Google has dozens of engineers working to improve every aspect of our service on a daily basis, PigeonRank continues to provide the basis for all of our web search tools.

Why Google's patented PigeonRank™ works so well

PigeonRank's success relies primarily on the superior trainability of the domestic pigeon (Columba livia) and its unique capacity to recognize objects regardless of spatial orientation. The common gray pigeon can easily distinguish among items displaying only the minutest differences, an ability that enables it to select relevant web sites from among thousands of similar pages.

By collecting flocks of pigeons in dense clusters, Google is able to process search queries at speeds superior to traditional search engines, which typically rely on birds of prey, brooding hens or slow-moving waterfowl to do their relevance rankings.

When a search query is submitted to Google, it is routed to a data coop where monitors flash result pages at blazing speeds. When a relevant result is observed by one of the pigeons in the cluster, it strikes a rubber-coated steel bar with its beak, which assigns the page a PigeonRank value of one. For each peck, the PigeonRank increases. Those pages receiv- ing the most pecks, are returned at the top of the user's results  page with the other results displayed in pecking order.

Integrity

Google's pigeon-driven methods make tampering with our results extremely difficult. While some unscrupulous websites have tried to boost their ranking by including images on their pages of bread crumbs, bird seed and parrots posing seductively in resplendent plumage, Google's PigeonRank technology cannot be deceived by these techniques. A Google search is an easy, honest and objective way to find high-quality websites with information relevant to your search. [2]

It's a name that both keys in to Google's academic birth, and hints at the masses of data that Google crunches every time we search.

Of course, you don't need to know the story to like the name. Probably most users don't have a clue. But for those in the know, it's a geeky story that gives the Google brand more depth, and more credibility. It's another sign of the authenticity that's lacking in other, more mainstream brands. One of the reasons for the media's scepticism of branding is that they believe it's all about fluff and no substance – and the corporate names invented out of nowhere seem to back that up. Google is one of a small group of young brands that have chosen names with stories behind them (Starbucks is another: Starbuck was a character in *Moby Dick*). Stories give a sense of history to something new, even a sense of soul. Another flash of humanity in a corporate world.

There are two other interesting aspects to the popularity of Google as a name. The first is that people feel free to play with it – I've seen people call it things like "the Googster" and "the Big G." This is a good sign: usually with a brand it's an indication that people feel so warmly about you – or at least that you're so familiar – that they feel like they're allowed to come up with their own versions of the name, just like they would with their friends and family. Think Bud, Coke, Macky D's (in the UK), Micky D's (in the States), MacDo (in France).

The second is one I've already talked about: that Google has made its way so far into our brains that it's actually become a verb. Natalie Woodhead, of digital branding agency Rufus Leonard, says, "It makes a good verb. 'Google it' is the friendly, workplace-way of saying, 'Ask mum.' Also, it always delivers; it doesn't reply, 'Ask your dad.'"

"To google" of course means "to look something up on Google." More specifically it usually means searching a person, and often a potential date. But it's something that makes a trademark lawyer shudder. Because while you might see it as flattering that your name gets such general usage (and spawns others, like Googlewhack and Google bomb), it can also mean to some extent that you've lost control of it. If times move on, people might apply "googling" to "searching something on the net using a search engine"; that search engine need not be Google. It's why in the UK people say they're going out to buy a hoover and come back with an Electrolux.

And of course, once it enters the language, and becomes not just a general term, but the generic term, there's another problem. The catch is that you can't protect generic terms in law. Your name could end up on the list of carefully built brands that land up on the scrapheap, with anyone allowed to use them – names like escalator, pogo and heroin – and that includes your direct competitors, leaving you with no brand at all. That's why companies like Rollerblade spend a fortune getting trademark lawyers to write to publications that use "rollerblading," asking them to correct it to "in-line skating." And as I write this book, there are reports that Google is doing exactly that. It has written to the author of the WordSpy website to ask him to note the word's status as a trademark. (That's the compromise that other brands like Hoover have had to put up with.) It's a tough line to tread, between fame and ubiquity.

A Google glossary

To google

To search the Internet for information on something (originally and usually using Google, and originally to find out information about a potential date).

Google bomb

(v) To deliberately manipulate Google's technology so that when certain search terms are entered, you are directed towards a particular site.

(n) An attempt to manipulate Google in this way.

Google dance

The period of the month during which Google updates its index of webpages.

Googlewhacking

A Google game, where a player must attempt to find a two-word search term (where both words are in the dictionary) that yields only one result on Google. It inspired the book *Googlewhack Adventure* by British comedian Dave Gorman.

Googler

Someone who works at Google.

The look and feel

Google is a pleasure to use. And partly that's because it spares us the visual assault that many brands feel obliged to inflict. Its pages give a sense of calm, thanks to all the white space. White space is the key to the success of Google's look and feel. Any graphic designers worth their black-rimmed spectacles will tell you that white space – in ads, documents, or webpages – says things are easy, everything's under control. It was one of the big early differences between Google and its competitors, together with the lack of pop-ups and banner ads. It also gives Google's site a decidedly oldskool flavor.

That flavor is reinforced by the way it presents the advertising it does have. It's in a carefully segregated area, and most importantly – it's just words. No whizzy logos, no flashing lights, no neon colors. Google claims that it is still very successful, because the advertising is so targeted to whatever it is that people are searching. But it also has the added benefit that there is nothing on any page to compete with the overall "Googleness" of it. Too often on the net brands cede control, and our attention as users, to third parties.

Where there is anything other than text, it keeps to the feel of the Google logo. Deeper in the site, there are brightly colored cartoons (but not too big). Google is a fun place to be, but it's not crazy.

Tone of voice

The way Google talks is an important part of its brand. Most of the time it avoids the business clichés and jargon you might expect of a 21st century, American, new media company. Its language is decidedly everyday, conversational. Glyn Britton of the Ingram Partnership says, "They don't talk down or up to us; they talk with us."

Take the "I'm feeling lucky" button. It's one of the things we see most often when we go to the Google website. Of course, it hopes luck isn't involved. The "I'm feeling lucky" button takes you to one result, and one result only. So Google is making a pretty big bet on the fact it'll have found you the right sort of thing. In some companies' hands, you can imagine the big promise, the rush of 0.18 seconds' worth of excitement … and then, well, hmm, no great shakes. A sigh of disappointment. An anti-climax. A moment decidedly lacking in luster. But the self-deprecation of the words "I'm feeling lucky" stops you being disappointed. Instead it says, "We know this is still an imperfect science, but let's look on the bright side. You might be surprised …." Instead of blaming them, you feel more like they're on your side. We're in this together. Bring on the results!

While Google might not be alone in this kind of relaxed tone with its users, most big corporations are shy of talking this way when it comes to an audience of investors. Usually people argue that that audience is impressed by professionalism and gravitas. No trace of fun is permitted. Nothing that seems too opinionated or personality-led is tolerated, for this is deemed to worry the investment community. It's as if we're normal people in the office, but tell us we have to talk to a shareholder or analyst and we get out the linguistic equivalent of a briefcase and pinstriped suit.

If there's one thing that Google is not about, it's briefcases and pinstriped suits. I, for one, really admire Google's ability to stay true to its own voice, no matter who it's talking to, and for me, Brin and Page's letter to potential investors at the time of their IPO is a masterclass in brand tone of voice. While remaining true to the personal, straightforward, conversational tone of the Google website, it is still credible, and utterly confident:

> Google is not a conventional company. We do not intend to become one. Throughout Google's evolution as a privately held company, we have managed Google differently. We have also emphasized an atmosphere of creativity and challenge, which has helped us provide unbiased, accurate and free access to information for those who rely on us around the world.
>
> Sergey and I intend to write you a letter like this one every year in our annual report. We'll take turns writing the letter so you'll hear directly from each of us. We ask that you read this letter in conjunction with the rest of this prospectus.
>
> Sergey and I founded Google because we believed we could provide an important service to the world – instantly delivering relevant information

on virtually any topic. Serving our end users is at the heart of what we do and remains our number one priority.

Our goal is to develop services that significantly improve the lives of as many people as possible. In pursuing this goal, we may do things that we believe have a positive impact on the world, even if the near term financial returns are not obvious. For example, we make our services as widely available as we can by supporting over 90 languages and by providing most services for free. Advertising is our principal source of revenue, and the ads we provide are relevant and useful rather than intrusive and annoying. We strive to provide users with great commercial information.

Many companies are under pressure to keep their earnings in line with analysts' forecasts. Therefore, they often accept smaller, predictable earnings rather than larger and less predictable returns. Sergey and I feel this is harmful, and we intend to steer in the opposite direction.

We will not shy away from high-risk, high-reward projects because of short term earnings pressure. Some of our past bets have gone extraordinarily well, and others have not. Because we recognize the pursuit of such projects as the key to our long term success, we will continue to seek them out. [4]

It's no accident that this declaration of policy came in the form of a letter – a kind of writing which is, at its heart, about one person writing to another. It is also no surprise that such a fresh approach to financial reporting caused a few ripples.

Most importantly, it is the voice of a company that knows what it is, and is not afraid to show it. It says: take us for what we are. What you see is what you get. In their letter, the Google founders acknowledge their debt to renowned investor Warren Buffett, of Berkshire Hathaway. Indeed they quote some of his words verbatim:

> We won't "smooth" quarterly or annual results: If earnings figures are lumpy when they reach head-quarters, they will be lumpy when they reach you.[5]

It doesn't mean that they always get it right, of course. Sometimes they too veer into jargon: "as a provider of services and moneti-zation for users …." And sometimes they can over-egg the corpo-rate hippiness: "At the Googleplex headquarters almost everyone eats in the Google Café (known as 'Charlie's Place'), sitting at whatever table has an opening and enjoying conversations with Googlers from all different departments." Maybe this is a hang-over from the feel of the Stanford university prospectus. It's the super-positive tone of someone trying just a little too hard.

Brand architecture

I hope you'll forgive me a few lapses into poncy branding terms over the course of a whole book. "Brand architecture" is a flashy way of talking about how the different brands a company owns fit together. Lots of companies end up with more than one brand – either because they invent new products for new customers, or because they buy them, or whatever.

Let's say I had a company called Taylor (I wish), that made, well, records, if I'm to get all my wishes in one go. Now let's say that I diversified into musical instruments; then making hats, and yogurt. I've got a choice. I could sell the instruments, hats, and yogurt under the Taylor name. Or I could think of different names for those businesses, so people on the outside wouldn't necessarily know they were all made by me.

These approaches have different advantages and disadvantages. It's probably going to be cheaper to call it all Taylor – I'll save on stuff like stationery and it'll be easier to work out contracts across the whole business. On the other hand, it could be dangerous. What if Taylor yogurt poisons people, or even kills them? Just by sharing a name, my other businesses might suffer. Giving them all different names will mean I can target them better at the different markets for those products, and it'll make it easier for me to sell the different bits of the business.

Good news for Tony Blair, though: there is a Third Way, a halfway house. I could give them different names, but make them look and feel similar. I get the best of both worlds. The different businesses benefit from an association to the good things about the rapidly expanding Taylor empire, while leaving me a bit of distance if things get tricky or I need the cash I'd get from selling them off.

.While branding experts like to present these three different attitudes to brand architecture as three separate approaches (usually described with words like "monolithic," "endorsed," and "freestanding"), most big companies end up with a mish-mash of all of them, or use different ones at different times, as they are in the process of bringing some brands closer to the core of the business, and pushing others away.

So, not surprisingly, Google does a bit of everything too. Most of its products (including the country-specific versions of Google) have descriptive names, and sit alongside a big Google logo. This is the call-everything-Taylor model (perhaps slightly more famous with brands like BMW). Google also owns some brands, like Blogger, that have no visual or verbal relationship to Google at all. And there are some in the middle ground. Froogle has its own name (even if it has deliberate echoes of its parent's, in a typically playful bit of naming), but it appears in the same primary-colored storybook style as the Google logo. To what extent this strategy is thought-through is probably, as in most companies, debatable. More likely, it's just what felt right at the time. But Google is left with a fairly typical pattern that helps it manage the "brand risk" of new ventures and acquisitions.

Chapter 4 ™

Google brand principles

The things we've been talking about here are to some extent the "tangible" aspects of the Google brand. The logos, the name, the language and colors are things we can see, if not touch. But the whole point of a brand is that these tangible elements provoke a reaction in users and potential customers – a reaction that's more emotional. So we develop a set of intangible associations that are triggered by the tangible ones.

Lurking behind all of these different elements then, there's a real sense of the Google personality, or culture, or philosophy, or brand – whatever you choose to call it. I prefer to think of it like DNA – what are the strands that make up the Google being? Or like seaside rock: if you broke the people and products in half (metaphorically, of course), what would you see running through them? I think there are several elements that add up to one big idea.

1. Irreverence and a child-like sense of fun

This shows up in their fooling around with their logo, even their name, and the impromptu hockey games that take place at the Googleplex.

From the point of view of an outsider, Google doesn't take itself too seriously. It even says, "We're not serious about anything other than search."[1] Of course we know that in the background, there's the serious business of churning through the gazillions of bits of Internet data to give us what we want, not to mention making money out of it. So we know Googlers are not daft. Nevertheless, they're willing to play. It's endearing because it's a very human trait. It's also a very brave position for a company to take. It takes a lot of trust: trust in your users' intelligence that they'll see you're good at what you do, despite the fact that you spend time mucking around. And it's a sign of trust in the employees – that they'll take this spirit and make the most of it, and not abuse it.

There's a paradox here, too. Because Google also says, "You can be serious without a suit."[2] It seems to be saying, yes, we play around, but don't underestimate us.

2. Sticking to search

It turns out, according to Rita Clifton, chairman of Interbrand in the UK, "In 19 out of 22 product categories, the company that owned the leading brand in 1925 still has it today – Nabisco, Kellogg's, Kodak, Del Monte, Wrigley's, Singer, Campbell's and Gillette among them." What's conspicuous about these long-life companies is that they are very closely associated with a relatively narrow range of products, and over decades they've delivered consistently good examples of those products. Of course we'll never know if they'd have done as well, or survived even, with different brands. But it's clear that the success of the brand is mostly down to what it's selling.

Many of the search engines, by contrast, have chopped and changed what they do, despite the fact that as a market, it's still only a few years old. Most, like Google, started out with a similar philosophy. Logically, the "best" search engine would be one that got you through its door and on to your real destination as fast as possible – a revolving door, in fact. But pretty soon they thought they were missing a trick. If you have millions of people speeding through your website, you have an opportunity to make money out of them. The trouble is, the quicker we left, the less time they had to sell us stuff. So, over time, the search engines' model changed.

Instead of trying to get people away from their sites, they decided to encourage them to stick around, by offering different products and services. Excite for example diversified into anything it could think of, to keep us on its site for a few extra seconds. Suddenly there were Excite fortune telling, Excite games, Excite online knitting (OK, I made the last one up). "Stickiness" became the holy grail. The search for stickiness turned the search engine model on its head. They became destinations rather than conduits.

We were sitting ducks. Depending on the search engines to use the Internet, we were an irresistible target for anything and everything they wanted to throw at us. With revenue as such a strong incentive, it became harder to see what these brands actually did, and what made them different from one another. They all tuned into amusement arcades cum shopping malls. Jez Frampton, Interbrand's UK chief executive, says, "The biggest Achilles heel on the web is the temptation to be everything to everyone." Frampton goes on, "Google has stayed true to its purpose, focuses on being even better at it, and never lets us down or confuses us."

Google founder Larry Page correctly called the situation in 1999: "Excite, Inktomi and Yahoo! are not really interested in search – they think it's a commodity, but that won't turn out to be correct."[3] He's since said:

> Ironically, toward the end of the 1990s most of the portals started as search engines. Yahoo! was the exception, but Excite, Infoseek, HotBot and Lycos began as search engines. They diversified and didn't take searching as seriously as they should have. Searching was viewed as just another service, one of 100 different services. With 100 services, they assumed they would be 100 times as successful. But they learned that not all services are created equal. Finding information is much more important to most people than horoscopes, stock quotes or a whole range of other things – which all have merit, but searching is substantially more important. They lost sight of that. It's why we started Google in the first place. We decided that searching is an important problem that requires serious concentration. That continues to be our focus.[4]

Instead, Google's stickiness was to its core philosophy of providing the ultimate search – a search that would know exactly what you were looking for, and give you back exactly what you wanted. As Google's Cindy McCaffrey says, "It seems counterintuitive to the concept of stickiness, but the point of Google is to allow people to find information as soon as possible and get on their way."[5] It makes its philosophy plain on the website, as another of its "ten things:"

It's best to do one thing really, really well.

Google does search. Google does not do horoscopes, financial advice or chat. With the largest research group in the world focused exclusively on solving search problems, Google knows what it does well and how it could be done better. Through continued iteration on difficult problems, Google has been able to solve complex issues that stymie others and provide continuous improvements to a service already considered the best on the web. Innovations like Google's spell checker and the Google Toolbar, which enables users to search using Google from any website, make finding information a fast and seamless experience for millions of users. Google's entire staff is dedicated to creating the perfect search engine and work[s] tirelessly toward that goal.[6]

Google is still frequently rated the quickest search engine, giving it a rather odd boast in business – people are leaving it in droves. While this approach didn't milk every user for all they were worth, it encouraged a different kind of stickiness – long-term loyalty. People came back several times a day because they knew they'd get what they wanted without the hard sell. Like the brands with longevity, Google has stuck to its core product. It's an approach that's impressed the brand consultants. Symon Sweet, brand strategist of Bluestone, says "It refuses to devalue the brand for short-term gain and is adult enough to realize that great brands are in the game for the long term. A rule from brand strategy, but it really does sort out whether the brand means business or not."

But it does leave Google with the question of how to grow, once the worldwide search market is saturated (which admittedly will still take a while). Google actually gets its employees to spend 20 percent of their time developing new ideas that don't immediately relate to what the company is doing now. Ironically though, it could be that Google's clear focus makes it harder to grow into other areas. John Allert, Interbrand's UK chief operating officer, says, "The more narrowly defined Google's brand proposition, the less 'permission' consumers will give it to migrate into other categories."

As we've seen, this is where Google has been quite canny with the idea of "brand architecture." Google has added, or plans to add, lots of features to its core web search function – hard drive search, a calculator, a dictionary, and so on. There are other ideas that even if they don't exactly follow the search engine model, are in line with a basic idea of "helping you get information," through the net or otherwise. These products are given descriptive names under the Google umbrella. And despite what Page says, Google does now own technologies that allow people to chat, or do other things unrelated to search. But these other ventures and acquisitions, like Blogger or the social networking site Orkut, don't appear to users as overtly Google products, even if we know it owns them. That way the purity of Google's Googleness isn't sullied.

Some of its recent developments and purchases – Blogger, Orkut, and Gmail – *do* increase stickiness in the traditional sense. At the moment search isn't sticky, yet that's where Google makes its money. But remember that Google wants to expand into lots of different areas of our computer; it wants us to download the Google deskbar so we can dip straight into Google, even when we're not on the Internet; in time, it wants us to incorporate searching our own hard drive; it wants us to use Gmail and let it search our e-mails rather than file them. It might not be a "stickier" approach, but it does give us ever more chances to Google.

3. Putting the user first

This shows up in not allowing pop-ups and not accepting paid advertising. This is another of Google's big claims, that forms part of its "ten things:"

> **1. Focus on the user and all else will follow.**
> From its inception, Google has focused on providing the best user experience possible. While many companies claim to put their customers first, few are able to resist the temptation to make small sacrifices to increase shareholder value. Google has steadfastly refused to make any change that does not offer a benefit to the users who come to the site:
> - The interface is clear and simple.
> - Pages load instantly.

- Placement in search results is never sold to anyone.
- Advertising on the site must offer relevant content and not be a distraction.

By always placing the interests of the user first, Google has built the most loyal audience on the web. And that growth has come not through TV ad campaigns, but through word of mouth from one satisfied user to another.[7]

To understand why this mantra, which is so apparently obvious, is so important, we need to remember what the world was like before we got to know the web. As the Internet blazed its way into our lives, it was pretty baffling for most people. Daunting, in fact. The gap between all the information there was out there, and how difficult it was to track down, could be scary.

As we've seen, the search engines, which arrived pretty fast, were the answer: they became an essential tool for novices like me to find our way around. And because they were essential to the way most of us used the net, they saw that as well as selling as their own products and services, they could make money from advertising while we were waiting for our search results. Not surprisingly then, they got cluttered with banner ads and pop-ups.

If we accept that search engines are something that the public came to see as an essential part of the Internet, it's not surprising people didn't want to feel exploited by them. Google correctly guessed that in time, the sell, sell, sell approach would annoy users. As Google's McCaffrey acknowledges, "If a searcher is waiting for something to download and then they get an advertisement, it's annoying. We offer great search results with no waiting time."[8] It's a principled stand that also makes long-term business sense. If you don't annoy your users, they keep coming back.

Not only did people perceive Google to be better at the job, but in comparison with the competition, it was just such a relief to get there: clean, white, uncluttered. It felt (and feels) so much better. Less brash, and less commercial.

This focus on the user makes Google *feel* as if it has less of a commercial agenda. I'd argue that its agenda is in its way just as commercial, but it's been brave enough and disciplined enough to see that this uncompromising focus on the user might cost it in the short term, but will in fact pay dividends in the long term. That's also the heart of branding theory. Ironically, by focusing on the user, Google has done the one thing it said it wasn't going to do at its inception: "build the brand." It didn't have to build the brand to the detriment of building a great product. But its founders' long-term view of the potential of their product, and their faith that putting the user's experience first was the right idea, has also built respect and loyalty in the eyes of their users. And what else is a brand for, other than to guarantee loyalty?

Public service searching

This focus, and this long-term view, has had another positive side effect for Google. I think people see it, as a result, almost like a public service more than a money-making business. The success of the BBC's search engine in the UK seems to echo the public's desire for public service search. In a recent survey, the BBC was in the top ten of search engines named by the public, even though its usage was nowhere near that high. It suggests that search is the sort of thing that we think should be provided as a public service.

The public service spirit of Google also seems to insulate it to some extent from some of the criticism that inevitably comes with the territory of being number one – and number one by far. Simon Waldman in the *Guardian* says, "as a result of its own ingenuity, and the tardiness of some of its rivals, it now holds something of a benign dictatorship over the net."[9] If Google is to be continue to be seen as benign, despite its enormous power, it needs to foster that sense of public service. But Google does have critics, and loud ones too, like Daniel Brandt of Google Watch (www.google-watch.org). He says, "Google is so important to the web these days, it probably ought to be a public utility."[10] As a regulator, though, Brandt is self-appointed.

This element of Google's personality also explains why the tide of the Google honeymoon turned when the media got a sniff of initiatives that seemed to fight against this quasi-public service personality. Gmail, Google's prospective e-mail service, will trawl through people's e-mail messages and then display advertising that relates to the words it finds (using the same mechanic developed in AdSense) in an advert zone similar to the one you find on the search results page. If we accept the argument that this feels like an invasion of privacy, it's made even worse by the fact that it's Google that's doing it. It's what we might expect of the supposedly ferocious capitalists of Microsoft, not the public-spirited citizens of the Googleplex.

The search for innovation

This desire to think of the user above all else also gives Google a responsibility to constantly find ways of improving our experience with Google. And that means it drives innovation.

Google needs to stay ahead of the game. It's trying to – at the moment it seems to be announcing and testing a new feature every week, or buying other companies that have technology Google would like to incorporate. I've already mentioned its 20 percent policy, which leaves its employees with a fifth of their time to spend on new projects that may or may not be related to Google's core offer, and may or may not be successful. It's a culture of institutionalized innovation.

The way Google communicates its innovation is revealing. It isn't shouty, brash, or boastful. New features and products tend to be introduced one at a time, through a simple piece of text on the homepage, unless you actively go looking for them (although the media will quite often make a big splash about them). So its innovations are presented as merely an expression of its commitment to a better product. To most of the outside world, innovation is not a prominent part of the Google personality, even if we might recognize that it is innovative. But it hitches its wagon of innovation to a higher purpose: better searching. Innovation is presented as a means to an end, not an end in itself.

Internally though, and to the really expert audience, innovation *is* presented as an end – hence the one-fifth policy. The company was built around an innovative technology, attracts creative people, and keeps them motivated and refreshed with exactly that message.

4. Honesty and openness

This shows up in clear labeling of adverts and its software principles.

> Google doesn't try to hoodwink us – it labels its adverts as adverts, and better than that, it makes its adverts useful.
>
> Glyn Britton of the Ingram Partnership

One of the most endearingly human characteristics of Google is its willingness to make the way it works transparent. It makes its money from advertising, but instead of promoting paid-for links in the order of search results, it labels its adverts clearly as "sponsored links" (although of course it would be even clearer to say "advertising"). Here's what Google says about it itself:

> Google is a business. The revenue the company generates is derived from offering its search technology to companies like America Online and the WashingtonPost.com and from advertising sales

based on keyword targeting. However, you may have never seen an ad on Google. That's because Google does not allow run-of-site ads that appear indiscriminately on every page of our results. Every ad shown must be relevant to the results page on which it is displayed, so only certain searches produce sponsored links above or to the right of the results. Google firmly believes that ads can provide useful information if, and only if, they are relevant to what you wish to find.

Google has also proven that advertising can be effective without being flashy. Google does not accept pop-up advertising or rich media ads. Text ads that are properly keyword-targeted draw much higher clickthrough rates than flashing banner ads appearing randomly. Google's maximization group works with advertisers to improve clickthrough rates over the life of a campaign, because high clickthrough rates are an indication that ads are relevant to a user's interests. To make it easier for smaller advertisers to take advantage of this highly targeted medium, Google introduced AdWords, a self-service advertising program that enables a business to display keyword-targeted ads within minutes, using only a credit card.

Advertising on Google is always clearly identified as a "Sponsored Link." It is a core value for

Google that there be no compromising of the integrity of our results. We never manipulate rankings to put our partners higher in our search results. No one can buy better PageRank. Our users trust Google's objectivity and no short-term gain could ever justify breaching that trust.[11]

Google has correctly judged that if it's consistently straight with us, then we'll trust it more. Honesty builds trust, and trust builds its reputation and our loyalty. Google's concern for its reputation, and our loyalty, shows that it cares about the principles of branding, even if it shies away from the dreaded B-word itself. Jeff Bezos of Amazon put it simply: "a brand is what people say about you when you're not in the room."[12]

Sergey and Larry's letter to Wall Street has the same candor (even if it does read like a list of pre-emptive strikes). It sets out, upfront, all the things they are going to do that will get the financiers' backs up: that they'll keep most of the voting power for themselves; that they'll avoid short-term forecasting; that they'll happily make risky investments if the potential reward is big enough in the long term; and ultimately, that buying a share in Google is a bet on them.

Again, as well as the disarming honesty, there's a satisfying consistency of tone across their communications behind the scenes to the investment community, and what they say to us mere users. A part of the Google corporate site talks about a set of principles they believe all software developers should follow (and which Google already does):

INSTALLATION

We believe software should not trick you into installing it.

UPFRONT DISCLOSURE

When an application is installed or enabled, it should inform you of its principal and significant functions.

SIMPLE REMOVAL

It should be easy for you to figure out how to disable or delete an application.

CLEAR BEHAVIOR

Applications that affect or change your user experience should make clear they are the reason for those changes.

SNOOPING

If an application collects or transmits your personal information such as your address, you should know.

KEEPING GOOD COMPANY

Application providers should not allow their products to be bundled with applications that do not meet these guidelines.[13]

Few corporations are so clearly driven by principles, or so open about those principles. The emphasis on openness is deliberate. When Google got embroiled in the debate about Gmail's supposed invasion of people's privacy, it went on the defensive – but in typically open, honest style. First, Brin recognized why people were somewhat skeptical about the service: "It's a high-quality product. I like using it. Even if it seems a little spooky at first."[14] But then he said, "Any web mail service will scan your e-mail. It scans it in order to show it to you; it scans it for spam. All I can say is that we are very up-front about it. That's an important principle of ours."[15] Page added, "you should trust whoever is handling your e-mail."[16]

Trust: that word again. It's at the heart of any great brand, but especially Google. Trust is of course the brand and business benefit that Google gets from its policy of honesty. It makes us like it, and it makes us, it hopes, more likely to stick by it in the future. But openly appealing to your audience's perception of you as trustworthy can backfire, as it did when Tony Blair squirmed his way out of a funding furor with the line, "I'm a pretty straight kind of guy." Raise people's suspicions too often, protest your trustworthiness too much, and they stop trusting you.

Of course, it's very easy to just say all this stuff. It isn't enough to say that you're open; customers these days can see through anything they suspect to be pure spin. *Demonstrating* that you really are open is more impressive. And "Google Labs" is one demonstration. It's an area of the site where the likes of thee and me can go and sign up to Google projects and products that are still in development. It asks for feedback, and of course, in a spirit of openness, makes it plain that these ideas are not yet running at their best. Not only is it open, it's also inclusive. It makes me as a user feel like I'm actually part of Google, and can do myself a favor by making it work even better in the future.

(I'm currently lending my computer's spare capacity to research projects that need a bit of extra computing power. Other tests going on as I write include Google's hard drive search and Gmail.)

But before all this gets a little too sycophantic, there are clouds on the horizon. Daniel Brandt of Google Watch is one of the biggest critics of the Big G. He is one of a number who believe the public face of openness and high-tech hippy-dippiness is covering up more sinister behavior, behavior that is using gizmos like the deskbar and hard drive search to store lots of information about me and what I look at on the Internet, for much longer than most people would deem reasonable. In the words of Jack Schofield of the *Guardian*:

> Did you ever search for information about AIDS, cancer, mental illnesses or bomb-making equipment? Google knows because it has put a unique reference number in a permanent cookie in your hard drive (which doesn't expire until 2038). It also knows your internet (IP) address.[17]

He also accuses Google of actively penalizing site owners who question Google's PageRank™ technology, leaving them plummeting down the very rankings they bemoan. Google Watch also believe it's Google's public perception as open that has allowed it to get away with all this.

There's no doubt that as Google gets bigger internationally, and more powerful, its spirit of openness will increasingly be challenged by the day-to-day running of the business, and the pressure groups looking for a helping hand (or to beat down dissenting voices). Google's ethical territory becomes increasingly grey, not black and white.

Google Watch believes one strong challenge to Google's openness came from the east. When Google found itself blocked by the Chinese government – thereby stopping 46 million Internet users from finding information critical of the Chinese government – Google said it was "currently working with the Chinese government to resolve the issue."[18] International diplomacy Mountain View-style means Google is now up and running in China again, with some links to searches on Tibet, president Jiang Zemin, and the Falun Gong spiritual movement removed. How open is that?

A similar furor erupted when Google removed links to Operation Clambake, an anti-Church of Scientology website, when the Church said the site was breaching its copyright. Here's what Brin had to say:

> The Scientologists made a copyright claim against an anti-Scientology site. It had excerpts from some of their texts. The counter-Scientology site, Xenu.net, didn't file an appeal. It sort of folded. Consequently, we were forced to omit their results, but we explain what happened on the search. If things are missing from a search, we often link to websites that explain the controversies. So now, if you do a generic search on

Scientology, you get a link to a site that discusses the legal aspects of why the anti-Scientology site isn't listed. In addition, this independent site links to the anti-Scientology site. As a result, if you search for Scientology, you will be armed with anti-Scientology materials as well as pro-Scientology material.[19]

It was a typically Googlish solution to these problems of apparent censorship: where links are removed in an apparently very pragmatic business "fudge," it finds a way to be open about its lack of openness and reinforces one of its principles.

These are various threads that make up the Google DNA – its playfulness, its openness, its commitment to search, its focus on the user and its spirit of public service. The founders have summed it up themselves, too:

Don't be evil

This is the closest thing there is to what the consultants would call an "articulation of the brand." It's a revealing line. Most companies express their central ideas in business terms – "the ultimate logistics solutions provider," "the ultimate shopping experience," and the like. Google's philosophy is less about business objectives, and more a moral code, a way of relating to the world. It's also very inward-focused; it's not about what it's going to do for users, simply how it's going to behave itself.

It's been said many times that brands seem to have become a replacement for religion in society – we put our faith in their consistency and steadfastness, and use them to identify and align ourselves with others. Advertising agency Young & Rubicam even went as far as to say "belief in consumer brands has replaced religious faith as the thing that gives purpose to people's lives."[20] If this is true, then Google is closer to a real religion than most, a throwback to an overtly moral or ethical viewpoint. Its founders are upfront about the moral principles that underpin their behavior. Perhaps they're not quite the child-like geeks we've been led to believe.

From our standpoint in the middle of Googlemania, it's easy to see why some people have asked, "is Google God?"[21] To its credit, Google recognized – and did so early on in its history – its potential for enormous popularity, and therefore power. After all, most websites now owe a big chunk of the traffic they get to a pointer from Google. I think we should be grateful, and perhaps a little relieved that, like Spider-Man, it realizes that with great power comes great responsibility. Brin and Page have said, "searching and organizing all the world's information is an unusually important task that should be carried out by a company that is trustworthy and interested in the public good."[22] As a result, it seems Page and Brin have created a company in their own image, a corporation built by people who are somewhat suspicious of corporations.

Or do you think I'm mad? Have I swallowed a bit of sophisticated corporate spin, hook, line, and sinker? It's true that "don't be evil," while bold, is vague. President George W.

Bush's talk of an "axis of evil" drew opprobrium from across the world, as a right-wing, reactionary, absolutist view of the world, defined according to his own dogmatic view of things. Why would a brand like Google – aimed at Internet users of all religious and political persuasions – want to wade into such sticky territory as the stuff of good and evil? My secret un-named new media source has a cynical view of Google's approach:

> I think a lot of people respect Google's resistance to plastering their own pages with "skyscrapers" and "leaderboards" – even if they offer them to other people. In effect they're offloading users' hatred of web advertising onto members of their advertising program, whilst appearing relatively saintly themselves.

The founders' explanation of their motivation is simply that they feel it's the right thing to do. And they own up to the problems with such a philosophy too, in an interview with *Playboy* that got them a lot of trouble at the time of their IPO.

> BRIN: As for "Don't be evil," we have tried to define precisely what it means to be a force for good – always do the right, ethical thing. Ultimately, "Don't be evil" seems the easiest way to summarize it.

PAGE: Apparently people like it better than "Be good."

BRIN: It's not enough not to be evil. We also actively try to be good.[23]

It starts with the boys themselves. For instance, they both drive a Toyota Prius, a car that runs on a combination of electricity and traditional energy. But the things that Google does to "actively try to be good" aren't that far from what many big corporations do. It has tried to nurture its relationship with the knowledgeable, techie fan base that did so much to establish its credibility in the early days. It launched the Google Programming Contest – offering $10,000, and a trip to the Googleplex. (Daniel Egnor, who won it, designed a way of searching webpages in a specific geographical area.) Brin says, "we have Google grants that give advertising to nonprofit organizations. A couple hundred nonprofits – ranging from the environment to health to education to preventing various kinds of abuse by governments – receive free advertising on Google."[24] Page adds, "We're also working to set up a Google foundation that will have even broader initiatives."[25]

These are fairly run-of-the-mill activities for any big brand with an eye on "corporate social responsibility." It's clear that "don't be evil" or "be good" (depending on whether you take your glass half empty or half full) are actually much more important as principles that underpin the way Google does its business. Page says: "The 'Be good' concept also comes up when we design our products. We want them to have positive social effects. For example, we just released Gmail, a free e-mail service. We said, 'We will not hold your e-mail hostage.' We will make it possible for you to get your e-mail out of Gmail if you ever want to."[26]

Even if "don't be evil" is a long way from typical brand statements, it's a very clear statement of intent, and a strong "central organizing principle," which is how Rita Clifton, chairman of Interbrand in the UK, actually defines a brand. In many ways it's a liberating principle: it says we don't have to play by the normal big company rules if we don't think it's the right thing to do, and Google's IPO is a case in point.

I think its philosophy has played a big part in what has made the public like Google, and made it the best-loved brand of recent times. But it's also a lot to live up to. To some extent if you set your flag on the moral ground, you're setting yourself up for a fall, and after the Gmail debacle there's some evidence that users view any suspicion of more "corporate" behavior – any signs of the "evil" Google talks about – more harshly than they would if it were any organization other than Google. Indeed, such an upfront statement of moral conviction makes accusations of hypocrisy and sanctimoniousness pretty easy.

And it also invites the question, who decides what's evil? Eric Schmidt, Google's CEO, once said, "evil is whatever Sergey decides is evil."[27] Page and Brin say:

> Somebody's always upset no matter what we do.
> We have to make a decision; otherwise there's a

never-ending debate. Some issues are crystal clear. When they're less clear and opinions differ, sometimes we have to break a tie. For example, we don't accept ads for hard liquor, but we accept ads for wine. It's just a personal preference. We don't allow gun ads, and the gun lobby got upset about that. We don't try to put our sense of ethics into the search results, but we do when it comes to advertising.[28]

It's disarming to hear Google admit that its moral absolutes aren't all that absolute. But the bigger and more powerful it becomes, the more it's confronted with problems like the Chinese blocking of Google, or the Scientology search debate. Its decisions are under ever more scrutiny and get ever more criticism.

These incidents do pose a problem for Google. It has described the way its technology works as "uniquely democratic." Yet as Google gets bigger it will be harder to square the circle of providing unmediated access to the Internet, and the interest of powerful "pressurizers" – the American right, the Chinese government, big business, or whoever might turn out to be crucial to Google's success or people's access to it.

There's even a paradox in the structure of Google itself. This is the company that came up with a unique process for its IPO to encourage more individual shareholders rather than institutional investors, a more "democratic" approach to keep them away from the path of corporate evil. Yet it also chose a similarly unconventional structure to preserve the uncommon amount of power of the "triumvirate" at the top of Google. You could argue that runs directly counter to transparency, democracy, and accountability, and limits the right of this base of individual shareholders really to influence decision making. It seems like a classic bit of Google – a big idea, a dose of humanity, and a somewhat contradictory moral position that bears the unmistakable stamp of the big boys at the top.

These different strands of DNA begin to explain a lot of what we like about Google. But we don't just like Google, according to Brandchannel.com: it's our favorite. I think it's the combination of these elements that really makes Google powerful, a brand that people will say they actually "love." Taken together, these ingredients lead us to other favorable conclusions. There's a whole that's greater than the sum of its parts.

1. **Google is unconventional, even iconoclastic.** The whole Google package makes for something pretty out of the ordinary. I suppose that's why Google sometimes ends up being described as "wacky," although I don't think it is. It's too clever for that. But it has managed to keep the feel of a loose gang of like minds, rather than a corporation. And for a long time it was the plucky underdog (and we all love an underdog – or is that just us British?), not afraid to play by different rules to the big boys; a little secret it was cool to champion; a character. Sometimes it even challenges its competitors directly (like when Larry Page openly criticized Excite, Lycos,

and so on for forgetting the central importance of search to most Internet users).

2. **Google is human.** Lots of the traits that Google wears on its sleeve – like its sense of humor and its honesty – are traits we normally associate with, and admire in, people. Think of the Zeitgeist feature (which charts the most popular searches at any given time), or the "I'm feeling lucky" button. These are not things that Google had to do to impress us or be taken seriously as a search engine. But it did them, because it thought they might be interesting or fun. Because they just felt right.

   While we might see other positive attributes in more typical corporations, they usually stand for something colder, more mechanical – qualities like efficiency, efficacy, or innovation. Ironically for a company that grew around a technological innovation, Google isn't presented that way. It's very definitely presented as the work of human beings, real people who have opinions, tell jokes, and draw doodles.

   "Don't be evil" is the ultimate expression of that. After all, it's a moral standpoint. And there is nothing more personal, and therefore more human, than a set of morals.

3. **Google is authentic.** If we accept that Google has successfully presented itself as human, it's part of a broader movement. This movement has been described as "authenticity," which is a word I've used a few times so far to describe what's different about the Google brand. Authenticity is about experiences that are more 'real' than the contrived, managed ones the traditional superbrands can offer. The brands that will

succeed in the age of authenticity are ones, like Google, that feel less spun, and more democratic.

This puts Google in sharp contrast to most of the big brands of the 20th century. Coke and their ilk were about simple things said loud: simple messages, repeated almost without change the world over, backed by powerful corporate machines. Even if their messages were about communities and global harmony, few of us saw the companies behind them as harmonious communities of people we'd like if we met them. We saw efficient commercial operations, producing consistent, apparently desirable products. This lack of humanity to the perception of the corporations made them easy to caricature. Naomi Klein's *No Logo* put the case against some of them: the fluffy face of ruthless capitalists, exploiting employees and customers alike.

If the 20th century brands are all about predictability – knowing we can rely on them for consistent delivery of whatever it is they produce: black liquid, computers, shoes – then Google's 21st century authentic business and activities are less efficient, less consistent, less predictable, but in a good way. The results of Google's product are also by their nature less consistent, less managed, more individual, because they are always a response to an individual inquiry. It's something we want, not something we're sold. We seem to like these more authentic brands, enjoy them, and trust them on a deeper level. David Boyle's book *Authenticity: Brands, fakes, spin and the lust for real life*, has charted the rise of authenticity as a 21st century consumer choice:

It is beginning to be clear that the dominant cultural force of the century ahead won't just be global and virtual, it will actually be a powerful interweaving of both opposite drives – globalisation and localisation, virtual and real, with an advance guard constantly undermining what is packaged and drawing the rest of society along behind them.[29]

Sounds almost like Googlish, doesn't it? Boyle also sees authenticity in a number of modern phenomena: the popularity of organic food, and farmers' markets, book groups, even unconventional politicians. He sees them all as a return to a more real experience of life, one in which the hand of humans is all-important. Google can clearly never claim to be as authentic an experience, as, say, growing a potato and eating it. But read Boyle's definition of authenticity:

Authenticity may mean natural or beautiful, it may mean rooted geographically or morally, but behind all that it means human. It means that the full complexity of people is recognised, that their need for human contact is recognised, that their uniqueness and individuality is recognised too.[30]

For a product that is based on enormous amounts of data, sifted automatically, electronically, Google nevertheless has made a big thing of its humanity. It has stressed the importance of human ingenuity in its stories, and has built a culture tuned to the human condition rather than rigorous business efficiency. It even has made the way it looks irregular and unpredictable through the use of the holiday logos. I asked Boyle if he would classify Google in his terms as "virtual real" – a real experience (getting the information that I personally am interested in) through a virtual system:

> Somehow there is something authentic about Google and I've been wondering what it is. I suppose it's virtual real in the sense that Amazon is – it provides you with something tangible (not something ephemeral – well, knowledge of a kind) and does it supremely well. If you compare it to what we had before Google, it's fast, accurate, doesn't overwhelm you with selling messages – it's just really really good. It treats you like a real person, rather than some consumer or selling opportunity – maybe that's what gives it that authentic sense.

Over a couple of days (virtually, via e-mail, of course), David Boyle and I talked more about where Google's sense of authenticity comes from. He added:

> The more I think about authenticity, the more I think it's about human-scale, human-shape, providing experience with texture – rather than glitzy shiny pseudo-experiences. And Google, I

suppose, gives you the lot. It doesn't assume things for you, doesn't try to automate things you don't want automated – it is actually a very human experience to use. And it's free of course, though I'm not sure that has anything to do with it. People also like the fact that it has stuck two fingers up to the financial world. That in itself may make it real!

Finally, on his walk to work, he came up with this suggestion: "I have a feeling the authenticity comes from the absolute sense of simplicity."

Boyle sees Google, Amazon, and ebay as examples of how the Internet can produce relatively authentic brands. When I asked him what Google could do to be more authentic, his answer was "fund libraries" – therefore bringing Google out of the virtual world and into a tangible space. I'd argue whether that would actually make Google more authentic. After all the end result of that experience is the same: go somewhere (online or offline), seek out information, find it, and maybe get entertainingly diverted on the way. In that sense Google is already as authentic as it needs to be.

You could argue that Google's marketing is more authentic than a traditional brand, too. Instead of advertising, apparently true stories are passed through word of mouth. Boyle says:

> It has avoided being a traditional brand – all glitz and no substance. It is what it is, no more and no less – and certainly by playing up the human

beings behind the company, it is using the authenticity wave very cleverly. But equally, telling stories about products is, I think, what authentic marketing – if there is such a thing – is all about.

Rob Mitchell of MitchellConnerSearson says, "Consciously or not, Google has taken a stand against 'image' and the trappings of over-marketed, but basically hollow brands. This 'anti-image' has inadvertently become the Google brand."

One interesting aside here is that in the age of spin, of "branded" politics, with consistently managed themes constantly repeated, going "off-message" becomes a mark of exactly this authenticity that people are looking for. Some commentators think the desire for authenticity has contributed to the success of politicians like Howard Dean in the USA or Ken Livingstone and John Prescott in the UK. This perspective puts the run-up to Google's IPO in a different light. The financial community was very liberal with adjectives like "shambolic" to describe what happened. Google was caught out in at least two major ways. First there was the publication of an interview with the founders during the "quiet period" which is required by US law before an IPO. The fact that the interview was with *Playboy* did little to reinforce their slickness credentials. Next Google was caught out for not declaring shares it had issued to staff, an incident that threatened to derail the whole process at the last minute.

Yes, in the terms of traditional financial PR, these were big slips. But as demonstrations of authenticity they were nigh-on flawless. Here were the founders now casually chatting to *Playboy* when they should have been keeping their traps shut, and now getting told off by the powers that be for giving freebies to their lucky staff. Both stories backed up Google's unconventional, anti-corporate brand. I'm not suggesting these incidents were stage-managed. But a brand manager with a bit of chutzpah couldn't have stage-managed them better.

4. Google is an international American

Like most of the big brands of the last century, Google is American, but certainly not in the same way. Those brands wore their nationality on their sleeve – they shared the same "brand DNA" as America itself: liberty and individual freedom alongside a melting pot community where we're all equal and have the same opportunity. They've aggressively sold their particular branded version of the American dream wherever they've traveled.

Here too, Google is different. It is of America without being overtly American. Its commitment to producing local versions of its sites is testament to that. It rejects the one-size-fits-all approach. This open, internationalist approach to its origins has protected Google from the backlash other American brands have suffered as America's political direction takes the shine off the all-encompassing admiration much of the world had felt for it until now. There is Mecca Cola, a Middle Eastern challenger to the pre-eminence of Coke, but no Mecca Search.

Chapter 5

Brands like Google

No brand is an island. No brand is completely unique. When the brand consultants come up with a list of values, it's pretty likely you'll share some or all of them with other brands. There are only so many good qualities to aspire to.

Think of your friends. If you stop to think about why you're friends with them, you'll probably come up with things you have in common, things you agree on, shared outlooks on the world or even shared moral principles. So in workshops, when people are trying to be clear about the sort of brand they want to build or become, I quite often ask them who their "brand friends" would be. Which other brands have something of the same spirit? If brands were people, who would hang out with whom?

I decided to have a think about Google's circle of brand friends, and where their connection comes from.

Yellow Pages

In product terms, it's the Google of a different era. Similarly ubiquitous, the Yellow Pages must have been a wonder when it first appeared: a compendium of useful information, designed to get you what you wanted as quickly as possible. Like Google, ads are paid for, but presented alongside each other for us to make our choice without undue influence. And like Google, it presents itself as friendly, easy, accessible.

BBC

A fellow brand from the world of the media (although Google argues that it's really a technology company, and that it's just the application of the technology that's taken it into the realms of the media). The BBC is much older, and quite a bit stuffier than Google, but they do have something in common. That Google already seems to share some of the BBC's public service feel, despite being recent and profit-making, is a big compliment to the way it has done things. This public service ethos is backed up by a sense of impartiality: the BBC reports the news unbiased, Google presents search results impartially.

Orange

Arguably another technology brand, Orange arrived in the UK and quickly made a big impact. Like Google, it wasn't the first mover in its marketplace, which is traditionally a big advantage in a new product area. But it made it to the top table by communicating emotionally, and by rejecting the overtly commercial approach of its main rivals.

Orange also has a very intuitive sense of its own personality, probably the legacy of a small, motivated launch team. Now it's facing the problems that Google could find itself facing in time: how do you carry on when the charismatic leaders, with their refreshing vision, have gone? Orange is struggling to stay distinctive as it grows internationally, faces pressure from a big commercial shareholder (France Télécom), and its competitors catch up with its ability to communicate engagingly.

Starbucks

Like Google, Starbucks is an American brand with a world outlook. It doesn't shout about its US origins in the way the American brand giants of the 20th century did, yet it too is taking the planet by storm. They've also both chosen names and brands built on stories, ready to be uncovered by the curious.

Starbucks, I'm sure, would argue that it shares a similar philosophy to Google's "don't be evil," with its commitment to sustainable development and fair trade. But the public and the media, it seems, are less willing to believe it than they are Google. Is that because it's on the high street? Or because we understand a little more about retail than the fine workings of the net? I suspect public cynicism to branding increases over time in any marketplace, and the net is still much less familiar and understandable to us than a shop. Google will probably find itself in a similar position in a few years.

Innocent

UK drinks brand Innocent is probably the one that's closest to Google in how it makes us feel. Just as Google is serious about search, and not much else, the same goes for Innocent and juicy drinks. It uses simple, fun packaging, and is keen to tell the stories of its headquarters – Fruit Towers, which, like the Googleplex, is similarly nondescript from the outside. These stories have similarly become key to its "mythology" of the brand. Until recently, it didn't spend much on marketing and advertising, concentrating on great product and word of mouth to do the trick. Not surprisingly, it also has charismatic leaders (it's even a triumvirate) who started small, surrounded by a gang of loyal friends. It's lucky these two brands don't make the same thing – they'd be almost impossible to tell apart. If these brands really were people, they'd probably both skate in, head to toe in this year's slacker chic. It just goes to show there's no such thing as an original idea.

The Simpsons

I was watching *The Simpsons* the other day, and it struck me how similar are the spirits of Google and *The Simpsons*. Both are American brands loved the world over for their quirky sense of humor, their intelligence, and their refusal to conform to the stereotypes of their respective industries. Both have at their core a kind of anti-establishment optimism and love of their fellow man and woman. Heck, even the colors are the same.

And surprise, surprise, Matt Groening, creator of *The Simpsons*, is a Google fan. He says, "It's not my homepage, but it might as well be. I use it to ego-surf. I use it to read the news. Anytime I want to find out anything, I use it."

Chapter 6™

Inside Google

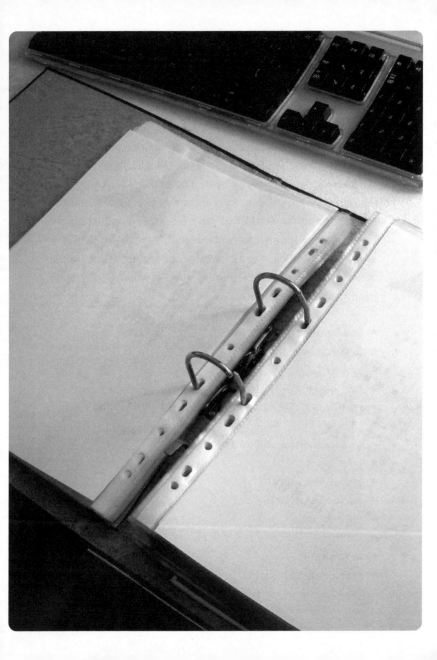

Google's headquarters have fascinated the media. The Googleplex is Google's home in Mountain View, California. Why should I care about its offices, you might well ask? Especially when Google is a virtual brand; all our interactions with it happen in the ether. It doesn't have shops, or anything like that. All in all, physical space shouldn't seem to matter to a brand like Google. Should it?

Paradoxically, the physical space that is the Googleplex (and the dorm rooms, garages, and offices that preceded it, and the offices around the world that have followed) is important in understanding the success of the brand. It's why people watch *Through the Keyhole* – you can learn an awful lot about people by what they leave lying around. Famously, what Google leave lying around are things like:

- lava lamps
- dogs running round
- scooters
- beer kegs in the garden
- the former chef of the Grateful Dead cooking the food at Charlie's Place
- toys lying hither and thither
- pool tables
- pinball machines
- hockey games in the yard
- doctors
- dentists
- beanbags
- exercises balls lying thither and hither

- a masseuse
- primary colors.

Now that I've fulfilled my contractual descriptive obligations, we can go on. (It seems to have become an unwritten law of journalism that you have to include in your opening paragraph on the Googleplex at least three of the above details.)

For a company that has spent hardly anything on advertising, it's no accident that the Googleplex has become so prominent a part of the Google story. Article after article has been written about the things that decorate the Googleplex, and what's happening there. (What is happening is all the secret googlings-on that make our hero the whizziest search engine on the planet.) We know much more about it than we do about other corporate headquarters (admittedly, there's much more to say). But the Googleplex has become a story because Google has shouted about it; indeed it has taken the media round on guided tours. In fact, it's even the star of one of the business principles from its website:

> **9. You can be serious without a suit.**
> Google's founders have often stated that the company is not serious about anything but search. They built a company around the idea that work should be challenging and the challenge should be fun. To that end, Google's culture is unlike any in corporate America, and it's not because of the ubiquitous lava lamps and large rubber balls, or

the fact that the company's chef used to cook for the Grateful Dead. In the same way Google puts users first when it comes to our online service, Google Inc. puts employees first when it comes to daily life in our Googleplex headquarters. There is an emphasis on team achievements and pride in individual accomplishments that contribute to the company's overall success. Ideas are traded, tested and put into practice with an alacrity that can be dizzying. Meetings that would take hours elsewhere are frequently little more than a conversation in line for lunch and few walls separate those who write the code from those who write the checks. This highly communicative environment fosters a productivity and camaraderie fueled by the realization that millions of people rely on Google results. Give the proper tools to a group of people who like to make a difference, and they will.[1]

They talk about it in interviews, too. Larry Page has said:

We think a lot about how to maintain our culture and the fun elements. I don't know if other companies care as much about those things as we do. We spent a lot of time getting our offices right. We think it's important to have a high density of people. People are packed together everywhere.

> We all share offices. We like this set of buildings
> because it's more like a densely packed university
> campus than a typical suburban office park.[2]

We don't just know what it looks like, either. We also know a little of what goes on there. We know that the employees (Googlers, they call themselves) have the 20 percent policy, developing projects that don't directly relate to their day-to-day work. Some of these projects end up in the rubbish bin; but some of them don't. Some of them go on to be surprise moneyspinners for Google, and to help keep them ahead of the game.

Google has been very clever in turning its offices into part of the Google story. It is canny PR that says, "This is how we treat our people, this is the home we've made for ourselves, so aren't we the sort of company you want to use?" As we saw earlier, it's very like the UK drinks brand Innocent, whose headquarters, Fruit Towers (actually an industrial building in dingy West London) and banana phones have also been put at the forefront of a brand story which the media, and eventually consumers, have been all too happy to pick up on, even if only a tiny, tiny proportion of them will ever get to visit.

Google is telling us about its office, and its HR policies, because it thinks it tells us something about the organization, something it'd like us to hear. And it works. Youssef Squali of Jeffries says Google's Sergey Brin and Larry Page had "undoubtedly bequeathed their entrepreneurial spirit and innovative nature to its employees."[3] It's in stories like this that we see that

Google is not quite as averse to promoting its brand as it might like us to believe. The environment of the Googleplex is one of the stories that lots of users know about Google, along with the founders' nerdy beginnings. It's become part of the mythology. And so not surprisingly the space, and the culture it contains, reflect the same ideas we see brought to life when we interact with the brand on the web: it's unconventional, irreverent, interested in people (and by all accounts, in the thrall of Larry Page and Sergey Brin: David Linsley of brand consultant Wolff Olins says "the culture and behaviour is famously young and 'wacky' even to the extent of being slightly forced and is often reported to tend toward the autocratic").

The story of Googlers spending 20 percent of their time on seemingly off-the-wall ideas similarly often gets linked to their reputation for innovation: Andy Hobsbawm, chairman of Agency.com, says "their culture of systematized innovation stems from [their] mission to create interactive services based on smarter technology and a better user experience. How the Google brand behaves is defined by our interactions with these useful, simple and brilliant online innovations."

Again, I don't want to suggest that these things aren't true – that the Googleplex isn't this fun, or that they aren't this innovative. In fact, they've created a culture to be proud of, and one which reflects their principles. But they've also certainly deliberately used these stories to full effect, and to build the Google brand. And who can blame them?

But apparently not everything in the technopark is rosy. As I write, ex-Googler Brian Reid has filed a complaint against

Google for "ageism." He claims he was told that he didn't fit into Google's culture of youth and energy. Google, for its part, strenuously denies the accusation. And I guess it depends on your definition of age. Reid is in his fifties, yet several of Google's senior management team are over 40 themselves.

Reid also claims that he was brought in because of problems there already were at the Googleplex. He says he was recruited "to correct some very serious problems ... with its workforce,"[4] talking about problems with management and the level of morale among women at the Googleplex.

Whatever the truth of the case, the Googleplex is still a place of work, and even a place of work filled with lava lamps must have its ups and downs. Susan Wojcicki, Google's former landlady, who left Intel to become a Googler herself, says Larry and Sergey "built Google to be their dream environment."[5] Clearly, the dream environment for two young male computer-obsessed entrepreneurs is not everyone's idea of heaven.

Chapter 7™

Great brand or great product?

Big brands are big business. Interbrand pioneered brand valuation, a way of putting a financial value on the "goodwill" of a brand. This value has been accepted to the extent that you can now show it on a balance sheet, and putting a tangible value on what had until then been thought of as a financial "intangible" has been a big factor in the rise and rise of the orthodoxy of branding. Suddenly there was a way of explaining the big gaps between the value of a company's assets and what the market decides the company is worth. There are now league tables of brand value (Coke is usually at the top). And there are awards for the effectiveness of brands or the quality of creative work that's used to represent them.

What's always worried me about these league tables and awards is whether they can really measure the success of a brand, as opposed to and separate from the success of a company, its products, or the way it's run. It's very difficult to judge this scientifically, or even objectively. There is no "control" experiment, where the same business is run twice over with different brands – which would let us really judge how important the brand is. Yes, a great brand can help you be successful, but it doesn't seem to be able to make you successful if the company's products or management aren't up to it. Not surprisingly, the marketing industry does not have awards for hopeless failing companies that nevertheless have come up with great brands. Jez Frampton, chief executive of Interbrand in the UK, admits it: "Great brands only prevail when they represent desirable products or services."

The question of what makes a "great brand" is important to this book, and indeed to this series of "great brand stories." Are

Starbucks, Guinness, Ikea, and Adidas really great brands, or are they the brands of great products and companies? The more I think about it, the more I keep coming back to that statistic about the brands that have lasted longest. Whatever else is true about them, most have stayed true to a core product, whatever fashions have come and gone: breakfast cereals for Kellogg's, razors for Gillette and so on.

For a while, though, it seemed like branding had become the first thing companies thought about, with what they offered coming second. I started working at Interbrand in the late 1990s, in the dot.com boom. We had a number of clients (usually under the wing of venture capitalists hoping to make a packet) who hadn't even worked out many of the details of what they were selling, but they felt sure that if they could just get a quirky name and a funky logo they'd be coining it in. Er, no. It didn't work. They didn't do very well.

Not Google. It didn't arrive spending millions on advertising. As we know, Google spent most of its time and money in the early days making sure the product was as good as it could be, and allowing an informed audience of techies to do the marketing for it, using good old-fashioned word of mouth. Google succeeded because it had a cracking product. People thought it was better than its competitors, and were happy to recommend it (and the explosion of the Internet was one of those few times when a whole new area of products opens up and people really are hunting round for the good ones, because they don't have any of their trusty old brands to rely on). This made it all the more convincing in the face of the mass of spin with no substance of the time. As the Google website says, "While the dotcom boom exploded around it and competitors spent millions on marketing campaigns to 'build brand,' Google focused instead on quietly building a better search engine."[1] And as other Internet brands come of age, they have started advertising in the more traditional sense – ebay is advertising on UK television for the first time as I write this book. Google still doesn't. Google's Cindy McCaffrey, vice president of marketing, says her budget is "less than 5 percent" of revenues. She says, "We don't need it." She says that in the early days, "we rang lots of advertising agencies, but none of them returned our calls."[2]

In a sense it's a return to a very old-fashioned way of selling: get the product right, and the people will come. Ironically for such a hi-tech product, it's almost a 19th century philosophy, and one that seemed to deliberately buck the branding trend of the previous decades. And Google professes that it will stay true to its core product. So if it's all about the product, stupid, can we really add Google to the list of great brands?

Plenty of brand experts remain unconvinced. Yannis Kavounis, partner in brand consultancy Onesixtyfourth, says Google is "the right product, at the right time. And it's a great, superior product. Same way iPod is. Same way Walkman was." Rob Andrews, creative director of branding consultancy R&D&Co, says:

> Google is a tool, not a way of life. It solves certain
> practical problems inherent in the Internet, but if
> it weren't available, I'd just use the next one. It

reminds me of a joke by Rich Hall – Coke and Pepsi, Pepsi and Coke. Between them they spend the equivalent of the GDP of a Central American country every year on advertising, and for what? I go into a store and say, "Gimme a Coke." "Sorry sir, we don't sell Coke, would you like a Pepsi instead?" "Yeah, whatever."

My secret source at the new media agency said bluntly:

It's a capable search engine that makes money from advertising without annoying the hell out of people. The concept of a company "standing for something" is just a conceit; a charity or a religious leader can perhaps claim to stand for a set of principles. A company? That's just crap. Perhaps Google have the common sense to understand that the best "marketing" is often a matter of giving people what they genuinely need with a minimum of fuss. The fact that their name has become synonymous with searching the Internet bears out the fact that they put product development ahead of self-promotion. What is being called "branding" is probably irrelevant – their logo could have been absolutely anything – a dancing moose or whatever. The search technology is where the intelligence and the utility lie. When it comes down to it, the word "brand" can

> be applied to anything. If Google took the logo off tomorrow and replaced it with a bit of plain Times Roman text (like they used to have), people might be a bit puzzled for the first couple of pages, but then they'd carry on using it just like they always had … people just aren't that stupid.

I think that's too simplistic. Yes, Google might succeed without its brand, but the fact remains that Google does have the main elements of a brand – a logo, a look and feel, a way of talking, and some fundamental principles – and they're now communicated consciously, coherently, and consistently. People cite these things as part of why they like using Google so much – so it's not just what Google does, it's also the way it does it that people respond to. And it does have a vice president of marketing. The Google brand is no longer irrelevant to the success of Google, Inc., if it ever was. So we can seek to understand how the brand has helped a superb product succeed, and ask if the role of the brand might change over time.

1. Google is a relatively "pure" brand

First things first. The Internet is a new environment for marketing products. The brands we're used to have some kind of physical presence in our lives. A can of Coke, filled with sweet, refreshing brown liquid. A shop with fancy sofas, and polite sales assistants. A car with shiny hubcaps and the smell of new leather. Even Internet-age brands have taken to offline activities to give their brands more depth in the real world. So you get online retailers opening real shops, and online art galleries opening up real world "showrooms."

For Google's users, on the other hand, it only exists in the ether. It can't rely on much to provoke a reaction in us – there's nothing to touch, or hear, or smell. There's no one we can meet for real to represent the brand. All it has is visual and verbal: the way it looks, and the way it talks. Andy Hobsbawm of Agency.com says:

> They are a very "low touch" brand. For search, their homepage is the only interaction of note and yet the character and personality of the brand shines through in the name and the logo, as well as the speed, simplicity and efficacy of their technology.

"Low touch" here means we don't have many different ways of interacting with that organization. Think of a bank, which by contrast is relatively "high touch:" we can walk into a branch, we can ring it up and speak to someone, it sends us letters, statements, we use cash machines, and we see its adverts on the TV. Or an airline: yes, there's a journey in the thing, but there's also how you book the tickets, where you get them, how staff treat you at the check-in desk, maybe even what car it sends to pick you up, if you're very lucky. That's a lot of chances to make a good impression on someone (and on the other hand, a lot of opportunities to screw it up). With Google, our only (jargon coming up) "touchpoint" is a few web pages. In that sense, it's a very "pure" brand, one where it was crucial at the very least to get the look and feel of the website right.

2. Google does market itself

Ema Lineker of Google said to me, "we don't promote our brand," and it's why Google wasn't, let's say, overly encouraging of this book. What Google says is true in the traditional sense of large-scale advertising and marketing activities. Indeed, Google has deliberately set itself up as an antidote to corporate marketing. So here's another Google paradox: as Rob Mitchell said earlier, "this 'anti-image' has inadvertently become the Google brand." Natalie Woodhead of Rufus Leonard says, "The fact that this long-armed brand spends almost nothing on advertising creates the perception that is just too cool for advertising, or that you've just missed the advertising and come late to it." Britton says:

> The Google brand shows up in their marketing, or lack of it. Brands aren't about marketing and advertising. Brands are about relationships between organizations and customers. Besides, what more than "perfect delivery every time" could Google promise in an advert? What channel could they use to get in front of more eyes than 41.6 percent of all US Internet users every day? And what better celebrity endorsement could they buy than Sarah Jessica Parker googling dates on *Sex in the City*?

Hayes Roth of Landor agrees. "With millions of hits a day on the Google website, it's arguable that Google itself is one of the world's best – and most perfectly targeted – advertising mediums."

It's a good point. Arguably it would actually be an incredible failure of the Google brand if it really felt the need to advertise its core product – given the sheer number of people who are using it already. The Google website itself is clearly a much more far-reaching medium to get its message across than most traditional marketing channels. Yannis Kavounis of Onesixtyfourth says:

> If you define marketing and advertising as the effort to promote yourself, create awareness and build brand loyalty, Google actually spend a lot of money. What better advertising than being in every single corner of every major city around the world or offering a service for free! You know how much these things cost?

3. The Google "story" is managed

The lack of traditional marketing activities is, however, more than made up for by the things Google does do. We've talked about the importance of stories to the Google brand. We know it's no accident that we know so much more about the Googleplex than nearly any other corporate headquarters. First, that's because Google has a good story to tell. But it's used its PR value to full effect, so that interviews with the founders nearly always draw on the unique ways of the Googleplex to illustrate the company's philosophy. The story of the founding, and the name, are similarly well known. They have used the company's mythology as expressions of the brand, and thus as marketing tools.

It's also likely that the Google brand will become more important as the company matures. In their early days it was the genius of the product that established its credibility. Since then, we've grown to associate that credibility with the recognizable elements of the brand – the name, the logo, the homepage. They become the seal of quality, or trust, or love, or whatever we feel for the brand. Now, if we stopped to think, it's probably difficult for us to know why we use Google rather than any other search engine. Are they still the best? Not sure. Am I used to them? Well yes, but I've been used to lots of products and still tried something new. But do I like them? Do I trust them? If the answer's yes, then that's a quality that is no longer intrinsically linked to the product, but belongs to something vaguer, and more abstract – the brand.

So let's imagine that a competitor emerges with a technology that is equally effective (some would argue that day has already come). Our initial reason for choosing Google then disappears. What it's left with, to try to guarantee our loyalty, is the brand. The fact that we like it and not just admire or respect it then becomes crucial. It's an emotional reason for us to keep coming back to it when the rational reason is diluted or disappears altogether. Reputation becomes crucial. So it does need to worry about its brand – what people say about it when it's not in the room – whether it chooses to talk about it like that or not.

Chapter 8 ™

Google future

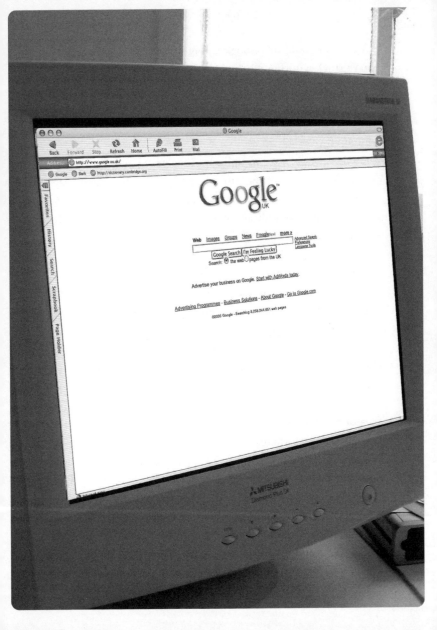

But hold on, hold on. Google's only existed for seven years. If you've stuck with me this long, and have maybe even accepted that Google could qualify as a great brand, you might still be harboring niggling doubts about its potential for longevity. Will Google really be one of those brands we're still talking about in a hundred years' time?

On the surface, it seems unlikely. Google is a young brand in a young market. An upstart that helped people find their way through a confusing new world of technology. That technology is going to change radically year by year, decade by decade. It seems unlikely that Google's category of "search engine" will even exist for very long in the scheme of things.

But the whole point of a brand is to help insulate your business from the tedious day-to-day ups and downs that the market, technology, and your competitors throw at you. Think of the Carphone Warehouse, one of the UK's biggest retailers of mobile phones. Its original category – carphones (big old clunky phones that put you in mind of matt black plastic bricks) – has disappeared, swallowed by a whole world of pocket-sized mobile phones, smart phones, and PDAs. And the idea of buying them in warehouses seems old hat too. Mobile phones are everywhere. Every high street in the land is full of shops selling mobile phones. So logic might tell you that a company called the Carphone Warehouse has had its day. But no: it's going great guns. All right, the carphones have gone. As have the warehouses, replaced by shops like everyone else's. But the Carphone Warehouse has succeeded because it built a brand, and not just a business that did "what it says on the tin."

Because people associated it with a friendly attitude and impartial advice, the fact that the name ended up as a red herring didn't seem to matter.

Maybe Google can do the same. If we like it enough, and the way it does things, maybe it could end up doing something entirely different and we'd still stick with it? (A brand consultant writes: this is called "brand stretch," and it's the phenomenon that gives you Virgin, a company that started off making records, selling you holidays, cola, heck, even wedding dresses. Or that leaves a company like Caterpillar, a company with years of history in the business of heavy industrial vehicles, making top-selling, er … shoes and jackets.) Ask Google what it's doing next, and here's the answer you get:

> What's next from Google? Hard to say. We don't talk much about what lies ahead, because we believe one of our chief competitive advantages is surprise. Surprise and innovation. Our two chief competitive advantages are surprise, innovation and an almost fanatical devotion to our users. Well, you get the idea. You can take a peek at some of the ideas our engineers are currently kicking around by visiting them at play in <u>Google Labs</u>. Have fun, but be sure to wear your safety goggles.[1]

Vague, isn't it?

But the long-term future of Google might not even matter.

Because even in the next few years, the future doesn't look that rosy for the Big G. It has a number of big things to worry about right now.

1. Staying the best

Fundamental to Google's success so far has been being the best at what it does. It's why we tried it in the first place, and if someone better comes along it's going to be tempting to try it too. It's going to be pretty tough for Google to stay at the top of its game. Hayes Roth of Landor says, "Google is driven by complex technology that needs constant investment and nurturing to remain competitive. Patents and processes are notoriously hard to protect in this area over time and great success begets great competitors." Of course we know Google has been busy gobbling up other companies so it can harness their technology to improve and add to Google's. The IPO has given it lots of money to keep buying, and to plough into its own R&D efforts. The signs are that it's pretty serious about keeping the crown.

You could argue that in the face of threats as serious as these, the brand is a fairly superficial thing to be worrying about. Google grew by deliberately eschewing brand-building and concentrating on the most fundamental thing: the product. And it's true that Google won't survive for long if a new technology, or even one of its current competitors, simply outclasses it. We're not stupid. No one uses gaslights now, however beautifully quaint and atmospheric we might find them. To perform to its best, Google needs to outperform its competitors, however search, and the Internet itself, evolve.

But the Google that's competing now isn't the fledgling Google that came up and pulled the rug from under the first movers. We switched to Google because it was so much better than the competitors, in terms of results, and the experience of using it. All the goodwill we feel, that warm Googly glow, is now connected to the idea of the Google brand – both its obvious expressions, like the name and the logo, and those that are less apparent, like its principles.

In the last chapter, we asked what would happen if the competition got just as good as Google. (As we've seen, some people think we're there already.) Will we swap? Some of us might – because we want a change, because we want variety, maybe even because we don't like to see anyone get too big for their boots. But in most markets, faced with a choice between two very similar offers, most people stick to the one they know best. It's inertia (and somewhat unflatteringly, when I worked with the energy industry in the UK, they called us conservative folk who wouldn't switch "inerts." It might as well have been "invalids," or "vegetables"). We're even less likely to move if rather than being kept there out of sheer laziness, we actually like the current product, which seems to be the case with Google. That's real loyalty. And that loyalty is why the Google brand has now become one of its key weapons. From being something it ignored, the brand might be the one thing that saves it.

2. Potential competitors

Pah, I hear you say. Who's scared? Google wasn't the first search engine. It's always had competitors, and they've left the rest standing. What have they got to worry about? Rob Andrews of R&D&Co says:

> It doesn't really have decent competition, and I can't see a rival product ever replacing it, but 20 years ago I would have said the same about directory enquiries. Whatever the next generation of directory is, it will have to be a big surprise to better what is here now.

But Google's phenomenal success, its worldwide appeal, a near monopoly, and its soaring share price must look pretty tempting to lots of potential challengers. Google itself grew because of the ease with which people can switch allegiance on the net. Brands like Alta Vista were in trouble almost as soon as Google came along. The naysayers say that the same could just as easily happen to Google.

Yahoo! has grown through the acquisition of search companies like Overture and Inktomi to become a serious rival in terms of search effectiveness. David Sowerby of Loomis Sayles & Co. says of the search engine market, "It's an expensive price of admission. [Google] is a company with a great mousetrap, but there aren't any barriers to another company building a better mousetrap."[2]

And we all know who's got a few pence from the sale of mouses to build that mousetrap. A company that was even in discussions to buy Google a while ago: Microsoft. Not surprisingly, Larry and Sergey weren't for selling.

Bill Gates's empire is developing a search engine. Chief executive Steve Ballmer said ominously, "we think there is still a great lot of innovation in the search space. We will catch up. We will surpass."[3] As I write, it's still a prototype, but a finished version is coming soon, including "graphic equalizers" to let people emphasize different aspects of their search, like recentness of results, or how popular sites are. When Microsoft announced that it searches 5 billion webpages, thereby bettering Google by the small matter of 700 million, Google upped the ante: it doubled the number of its searched webpages to around 8 billion. Who knows what number Microsoft will be shouting once it's come out of testing?

All in all, it's shaping up to be quite a battle. The real danger for Google, though, comes not from Microsoft managing to index slightly more material than Google. After all, for most of us, our understanding of the technical workings of a search engine is fairly negligible, so the number of pages indexed probably doesn't vex us very much. No, a much bigger worry is how Microsoft might tempt us to use its search engine, and not anyone else's. Speculation is rife that Microsoft is likely to bundle its technology with the next generation of Windows. Ring any bells? It should. Like Google to search, in the world of Internet browsers, Netscape used to be number one: popular, good at its job, just the kind of brand you'd think we'd like to have around. That is until Microsoft began bundling its own web browser into Windows. Netscape's supremacy crumbled. It didn't even seem to be that people particularly preferred Microsoft's Internet Explorer, it was just that Microsoft made it so easy. It was sitting there, waiting to be used. Explorer became the Windows default browser, and people took the easiest route. It seems once people had to choose to opt out of Microsoft's version, they couldn't be bothered. Microsoft's bundling of Internet Explorer with Windows has caused a bit of a furor with competition authorities across the world, with rivals claiming its near-monopoly on operating systems gives it an unfair advantage in the browser wars. Even where those authorities have taken action (the EU fined Microsoft €497 million), for a company the size of Microsoft, it feels a little bit like too little, too late.

So will the same happen to Google? Will we all keep choosing Google over an easier option? Or will that little extra bit of effort deal it a body blow? Well, it's true that it's getting its defence in early. By getting us used to the Google deskbar and services like hard drive search, it's trying to get us to see Google as intrinsic to the smooth running of our computers before big bully boy Microsoft can muscle in on the party. And it's not just the big boys who are at it. There are also new smaller competitors like Blinkx, Copernic, X1, Enfish, already being labelled "the new Google," ready to take it on with new ways of doing search.

The brand is a key defence, and that's why it will become more and more important to the company. We do strange things for brands we love. I recently ran a workshop for a football club in the UK, designed to get its fans' opinions on some work it was doing on its brand. One fan left work early, drove for five hours to get to the workshop, and took part for an hour and a half (and didn't say too much, to tell you the truth) before driving the five hours back, without being paid by the club, or even given his expenses. But he did it because he felt it was so important to have a say in, or least see what was going on in, his favorite club. Admittedly, football clubs are fairly extreme examples of love and loyalty, which is both a blessing and a curse for the people managing those brands. But the point of branding is to inspire something of that kind of a reaction. The point is to convince us about something on an emotional level so that it overrides our rational decision making. If Google can get us to love it enough, then it stands a choice of hanging on to us in the face of something more convenient.

As we've seen in this book, it's going about it the right way. Most of us have an unusually warm and fuzzy relationship with Google, Interbrand says it's our best-loved brand, and many of us visit it many, many times a day. We already rely on it when, if we stood back and thought for a moment, we might rationally decide that we didn't really need it. (Remember that many people find the BBC's site by typing BBC into Google, rather than trying bbc.com.) What we learnt from the fall of Netscape was that people didn't like it enough to persuade them to go back there when it got more difficult. I think the strength of the Google brand means that's much less likely to happen to Google.

But of course, there are things that could happen to the business that would threaten the brand itself.

3. Keeping the focus

Google has been pretty ruthless in staying true to what it sees as its core business, and it's something that has set it apart from many of its historic competitors. But there's something of a haphazard tendency at Google too. Arguably, haphazardness is somewhat hard-wired into the DNA of Google; it's a natural consequence of asking people to spend a fifth of the time doing things outside the day-to-day remit of their jobs. It's creative. It's refreshing. It must be exciting. But is it what users really want?

Gmail and Froogle are results of the one-fifth policy. The Internet is also buzzing with rumors that Google is developing its own web browser, having poached a number of Microsoft employees who worked on early versions of Internet Explorer, and having registered gbrowser.com as a name. We could take the Google line, seeing these ideas as simply giving people new ways to use the net, or their computer, a natural extension of what Google's about. The alternative view is that these are beginnings of a worrying trend: a Google that is edging away from its core area of expertise, confusing its users by introducing different products, or worse, scaring and annoying them (even to the point of building gmail-is-too-creepy.com). Yes, they have different names, but they feel like Google "sub-brands." They look similar, you get to them through the Google site, and the media has thrust them into the public eye.

This opens Google up to the potential dilution of the brand, and of its reputation for quality. Andy Hobsbawm of Agency.com says, "there's a danger if the company diversifies its strong name too far into things that it is fundamentally less good at or less in control of than the thing with which it started." Glyn Britton says, "the only real threat to Google will come from itself. I already get the feeling that they are a bit bored, and now they are well funded too they are starting to make too much stuff."

Natalie Woodhead of Rufus Leonard says, "Google can sustain its success if it puts more effort into doing what it does already, *better*, rather than trying to do *everything* better than everybody else."

Despite the speed of change in the sector, the company is resolute that the idea that underpins it is not up for grabs. It stands for one great product, like the Kelloggs and Gillettes of the world. "Our plan is to be a search engine," says Susan Wojcicki, Google's director of product technology. Of course, the kind of search engine it is to be can evolve and change. It has already launched Google Print, to search the text of books and then link to booksellers; Google Scholar, to trawl through academic papers; the deskbar; and we know hard drive search is coming. All of those innovations seem to sit comfortably with the idea of being a "pure" search engine. Google has used principles of brand architecture to distance some of its areas of diversification – Froogle, its price comparison package, Gmail e-mail, and Blogger – from its main heart. It means that if they don't work or decline in popularity, they can be quickly ditched without the main brand being damaged or losing face.

The fundamental question here is whether you see Google's core product idea as linked to our current perception of a search engine, which is quite likely to disappear in a few years, or something broader, something like "helping you get the most out of the sources of information open to you." At the moment, those sources of information might be on the Internet, but Google is spreading out of the online world. It has already added books and academic papers. Authenticity expert David Boyle raised the intriguing possibility of Google funding libraries in the real world. In fact, that's a logical extension of the Google brand, and it's an area of life – certainly in the UK – that does need a lot of investment; libraries simply don't seem to have enough books. Google needn't just fund libraries; it could run them. The Googleplex has shown us that it's good at creating fun, relaxing, creative environments while encouraging good work in them. It could take that same philosophy into the public sphere: schools are an obvious place for Google libraries. You can imagine shelves of books on a particular subject, perhaps with commercial adverts or brochures at the end of each one – a physical interpretation of the Google "sponsored links" bar on the side of the results page. Maybe this is the sort of thing the Google Foundation should be looking at to reinforce Google's credentials as a source of information, as a good citizen, and to give a greater depth of experience to the Google brand in the light of challenges from corporate behemoths like Microsoft. Larry Page and Sergey Brin have said that they would like the Google Foundation to eclipse Google in terms of its influence and impact around the world. Here's a way to do it.

4. Keeping the faith or selling out

But it's not just a question of sticking to its business strategy. It also needs to stick to the feel that's made it popular. I agree that the biggest danger to Google comes from inside. So far, it seems to have grown remarkably smoothly, from a few technophiles in California to a company with thousands of employees and offices all over the world (and it's put the good Dr Eric Schmidt in place with that specific mission).

But we've seen how Google's brand has more than a pinch of the irreverent, the iconoclastic, the unconventional. How irreverent and iconoclastic can you be when you become the mainstream? David Linsley of Wolff Olins says:

> It felt like an underground, alternative creation –
> the underdog that made it easy for us all to cham-
> pion – to replace the phrase "to search the Internet"
> with "to Google." The vernacular has now become
> mainstream to the point where Internet surfing has
> been replaced by googling (regardless of the search
> engine you use). Also, its burgeoning monopolistic
> status is leading it into some tricky territory. A
> brand that was once perceived as the antithesis of
> Microsoft is now being tarred with the same brush.

Rob Mitchell of MitchellConnerSearson says:

> Google resolutely refuses to act like a big brand or
> oversell itself, but has become a huge brand in the
> process. It's very hard for any brand (especially one
> that grows) to stay true to itself: just when is Google
> making too much money from what it does? When
> is an ad too overt? These are tricky things.

Glyn Britton says:

> The botched announcement of Gmail (or rather
> the content-specific ads within Gmail) showed
> that perhaps Google is starting to get a bit clever
> for its customers, and nobody likes a smartarse. I
> fear that the perfect balance they have managed to
> sustain so far between human intimacy and
> unimaginable scale is so fragile, that it is beyond
> any growing company in corporate America to
> sustain the brand.

In short, Britton thinks that Google might be leaving its customers behind.

We need to remember that at the moment, the philosophy and principles of the founders still infuse the way the company works; indeed, they've made sure by way of their unconventional voting structure, that even as they went public they managed to maintain the unusually strong influence of the duo at the top.

But what happens if one, or both, of them leave? If they decide after ten years that it's time to get off the Google treadmill? It's a tricky time for any brand. It loses a link to its history. And of course, while the brand is built around the charisma of two people, it is bound to end up somewhat human, authentic. When these people go, the temptation is for the organization to "tense up," to start to behave more like a corporation acting in the interests of its shareholders rather than the customers the founders really cared about.

It's a pattern repeated in many great brands. I've done lots of work with Orange, the mobile phone network. Like Google, it arrived in a developing market with a unique point of view and a strong personality: bold, brave, human. Now, with the founders gone, international operations, and a new owner in the shape of French state giant France Télécom, it's a company that feels like it has only a "folk memory" of the ground-breaking Orange personality. In a market that has grown up (and with competitors that have caught up), Orange seems to know what it should be like, but not quite how to do it. Or take a brand like Virgin, so successful as a challenging, consumer-championing brand in markets like airline travel, but that loses its way when licensed to EDF (coincidentally, perhaps, another French state-owned utility) to sell electricity in the UK.

Often the further these brands go from their roots, the less sure of themselves and their roles they become. As consumers, we can spot this lack of confidence, or lack of conviction. And just as a political party that loses its drive loses its voters, so we consumers vote with our feet and leave these brands. Symon

Sweet of branding and design agency Bluestone recognizes the danger if the brand is seen to "sell out:" "The biggest threat could actually come from its own users. People like to be associated with success. If Google starts to falter, its fan base may start looking elsewhere."

That doesn't mean that if Google has a few off-years, it's dead and gone. In Hobsbawm's words "most leaders fail at some point. Think Apple. Then they got it back together again." And Apple is indeed a case in point. A small, if influential, brand in its early history, after not very long (and the exit of one of its founders) it was in trouble. Its products were less innovative, and its results terrible. For a while it looked like another potential victim of the Microsoft squeeze. The return of its founder signaled a return to the spirit that had made it successful – creativity, fun, and above all, a sense of humanity at the heart of technology – and led to groundbreaking products like the iMac and iPod, products that have smoothed the company's way back to profitability and popular success. The challenge for Google would be to do the same if the founders stayed at home.

Chapter 9 ™

So what?

So is Google a great brand? Well, I think so, but I'll have to explain what I mean by that. Even if you agree, you might be sitting there thinking, what's so difficult about that? They did it all themselves, on the fly. Do I really need lots of highly paid brand consultants?

It's true, some of the highly paid brand consultants I talk to are still convinced that Google is a fluke, and unconvinced of its greatness. Instead, they see a room full of nerdy engineers, who set out to make a bit of clever software, didn't think about how to market it – in fact, decided to ignore marketing it – yet have accidentally stumbled on the most popular brand of our time.

But the fact remains that they *have* created a great brand. Maybe they didn't set out to, but that's what they've done. They decided to build the best search engine, and along the way they've had to make decisions about the elements of their business that usually fall under the remit of branding or marketing – things like the logo and the design of the homepage. Yes, they might have done those things fairly instinctively. But their instincts were good ones: instincts borne of their own personalities, their view of the world, even their own morality. They've since had to sum up part of that (*articulate* it, the brand consultants would say) through the phrase "don't be evil," and the principles it stands for. "Brand" is really only a shorthand for those elements working together, so it's no surprise that the personality of the brand they've created is a reflection of their own. The Google brand has been successful because they have ended up communicating the purpose of their product alongside an engaging personality, even if it was nothing more complex than "make the best search engine, without taking ourselves too seriously, or doing evil along the way." They've got that message across both to their own people inside the company, as well as to the rest of us in the outside world.

The fact that there was no "branding" process doesn't disqualify Google as a great brand; in fact, it makes it a more interesting example to study. If the purpose of a brand is to be the likeable face of a good product, Google must be the best modern brand, because it's apparently the one we like most. It has emerged naturally, instinctively. I'd argue that that is part of why it has been so successful – people recognize that it is less artificial, more authentic than many modern examples of branding, which are little more than exercises in corporate spin. Google has succeeded because the leaders behind it are the authors of its spirit, and truly believe in it.

Google has approached the whole thing pretty intuitively: no focus groups or brand matrices. Think of it like calligraphy. It takes great skill, but you'll never be good at it if you think too hard about it. If you're thinking too hard, it always shows – you can "see the working." The great calligraphers write quickly, instinctively, with confidence – and the awareness that such a risky approach sometimes fails.

Sergey Brin and Larry Page have taken the calligrapher's approach to their brand and their business. Time and again they have done what they believe to be right, even if the world around them was skeptical, or playing by different rules. They've tried to remain true to their own principles and build a brand that reflects them. If you'd been asked to design a number one search engine brand, through the logical analytical tools of gap analysis and the like, it's unlikely you'd have come up with anything like Google. But it works. And it's not a model that's easy to replicate, unless you happen to have the same confidence as the Google Two and the same beliefs.

That's not to say there aren't things that any brand, business, or organization could learn from the surprising success of our friends in Mountain View. It also doesn't mean you have to be an entrepreneur in your twenties to learn something from Google that you can apply. Sitting here with 20/20 hindsight, you can identify the lessons that are there for the learning, and ideas that are there for the pinching.

1. You can't have a great brand without a product people want

Make or provide rubbish, and you can have the most beautiful logo in the world or the smiliest staff and still the people won't come (or at least they won't stay). The success of the Google brand is underpinned by a fantastic product. When it appeared on the scene, slowly, most people's first contact was a recommendation from someone they trusted, followed by a good experience of the product. It was quite a starting point.

2. Word of mouth is better than advertising

Google's early success was based on recommendation from an expert group, and recommendation from a trusted source. This established the brand's credibility in the marketplace, and studies have shown that a credible recommendation sways us much more then advertising or scientific surveys. It also helped Google's credentials as a more authentic, unspun brand – using real people to sell rather than big media campaigns.

3. Be clear about what you stand for

Google did this first in product terms. It was clear that it wanted (and still wants) to be as close to the perfect search engine as it can be. That's a simple but challenging goal for the hundreds of people working behind the scenes at the Googleplex.

But you also need to be clear about the way you're going to do business. That helps you decide which things you'll do and which you won't. Very often this comes from a strong, motivational vision from charismatic founders and leaders. Sergey Brin and Larry Page's philosophy of "don't be evil" (and the thinking that lies behind it) has shaped much of what Google has done – from the way it treats advertising, to the way it treats its staff, to the way it handled its IPO.

4. Stick to your guns

Clarity in what you're about can give you tremendous confidence. It's certainly let Google do things the Google way and not the way everyone else does them – think of the IPO, or its commitment to improving search when the other search engines were desperately looking for other revenue streams. Google's legion of worldwide fans have interpreted this commitment as a sign of integrity which has earned it trust.

5. The brand and the company are the same thing

One of the questions I asked was whether Google was a great brand, or just the brand of a company with a great product. I don't think it matters. Where the company has one main product, its brand and that of the company become synonymous. In fact, to be successful, they need to be.

Some businesses talk about their "brand"; others talk about their "reputation" or "culture"; yet more might talk about their "philosophy," "spirit," or "mission." To me, these are all just different ways of talking about the same thing – not what you do, but the way of doing business we talked about in number 3, and the way it affects people – just expressed through different filters. At its most basic, it's as simple, and as important, as the heart and soul of an organization. Or perhaps what Rita Clifton, chairman of Interbrand in the UK, calls a "central organizing principle." I'd call them "central principles"; it's usually not as straightforward as one single idea.

Google's is unusual in that its central principles include elements that are unashamedly "moral," and this has probably contributed to the degree to which its users and employees feel loyalty to the company: it's easier to be loyal to something that is about human behavior than to abstract corporate philosophy. Its principles come through in its logo and the design of its website, but the same things are reflected in different ways in the way it talks (to both users and investors), the feel of its headquarters, even the way its product works. Google is a great brand (and a great company) because what we see on the outside matches what happens on the inside. Its brand is true.

Typically, in fact, the language that different organizations use to talk about these kind of ideas tells us most about who's pushing them internally, and where their power base is within an organization. When the ideas come from the very top, they're often described as "vision," "the Google way," "the Orange way," even "the Branson way" or whatever. If HR or personnel have a role in shaping this vision, people talk about as being the company's "culture" or "spirit." When marketing get the ball, they call it "brand." In fact using the language associated with just one of these small empires within an organization – culture, brand, and so on – can actually make the "central principles" less likely to be accepted across the board; to make them less central, in fact.

Branding is rightly criticized as duplicitous spin when it does-n't reflect the truth of an organization, when it really is a surface layer designed to manipulate us. Great brands reflect a core belief that's backed up in action as well as image. That's why there's such a correlation between strong companies and brands, and strong leaders.

6. Think long term

Google's history is one of thinking of the long game, and then reaping the benefits later. It's built the brand slowly by sticking to a clear set of principles. These principles might have cost it money or deals in short time, but they have bought it long-term loyalty from Google fans, and financial reward from the markets.

7. Try things, but keep them at arm's length

Google is diversifying into things that are outside the core idea of search, but it's being careful that if they stray too far, they don't sit obviously under the Google umbrella. By maintaining Blogger, Orkut, Picasa, and so on as brands in their own right, Google is also protecting the main brand. It's making sure that people are still clear what Google is, not baffled by an ever-increasing array of apparently unconnected services. That was the mistake many of its competitors made in the early days when they turned themselves into portals.

Google is a great brand. At the moment, perhaps the greatest. And that's simply because we love what it does, and the face it presents to the world seems to be an open reflection of what's going on inside, and what its people really believe. We like who we think they are. They're not hung up on the word "brand" or the activities of branding. They haven't over-thought it. Instead, they simply see these things as another expression of their philosophy, like the product is, and like their headquarters are.

But they've had it easy for a long time now, and things are changing. Like it or not, what we think of them – as a company, and therefore as a brand – is important now. It's not just all about the product, like it was in the beginning. If they do it right, it could play a big role in stopping them getting knocked off their perch, by either the giant of Microsoft, or another gang of plucky little guys trying their luck.

There are signs that what we think of Google is changing, with Google's techie heartland exploring other technologies, and the public being led to suspect its motives. It could be the start of a turn in the tide, or it could be a blip. But it will make the difference to whether Google is still a great brand in ten years' time.

REFERENCES

1. What's so special?

1   *Linux Gazette*, November 2000.
2   *Guardian*, September 5, 2002.
3   *Daily Telegraph*, August 1, 2004.

2. Google beginning development

1   *Playboy*, September 2004.
2   *Guardian*, December 4, 2003.
3   Google.com website, January 3, 2005.
4   Google.com website, January 3, 2005.
5   *Playboy*, September 2004.
6   Google.com website, January 3, 2005.
7   *Observer*, November 9, 2003.
8   *Playboy*, September 2004.
9   BBC News Online, October 2004.
10 *Guardian*, November 25, 2004.
11 *Playboy*, September 2004.
12 *Wall Street Journal*, August 17, 2004.
13 *Guardian*, April 1, 2004.
14 http://www.albinoblacksheep.com/text/victories.html, January 3, 2005.
15 http://www.coxar.pwp.blueyonder.co.uk, January 3, 2005.

16 Google.com website, January 3, 2005.
17 *Guardian*, August 24, 2004.
18 *Wall Street Journal*, August 17, 2004.
19 *Wall Street Journal*, August 17, 2004.

3. Google brand basic elements

1 *Financial Times*, March 30, 2004.
2 Google.com website, January 3, 2005:
   http://www.google.com/technology/pigeonrank.html
3 Google.com website, January 3, 2005.
4 Google.com website, January 3, 2005.
5 Google.com website, January 3, 2005.

4. Google brand principles

1 Google.com website, January 3, 2005.
2 Google.com website, January 3, 2005.
3 *Business Week*, September 29, 1999.
4 *Playboy*, September 2004.
5 *Financial Times*, March 30, 2004.
6 Google.com website, January 3, 2005.
7 Google.com website, January 3, 2005.
8 *Financial Times*, March 30, 2004.
9 *Guardian*, February 27, 2003.
10 *Guardian*, September 5, 2002.
11 Google.com website, January 3, 2005.
12 *British Industry*, September 2004.
13 Google.com website, January 3, 2005.

14   *Playboy*, September 2004.
15   *Playboy*, September 2004.
16   Channel 4 News online, August 27, 2003.
17   *Guardian*, January 8, 2004.
18   *Guardian*, September 5, 2002.
19   *Playboy*, September 2004.
20   FT.com, July 29, 2004.
21   SearchEngineWatch.com, October 16, 2003.
22   *Playboy*, September 2004.
23   *Playboy*, September 2004.
24   *Playboy*, September 2004.
25   *Playboy*, September 2004.
26   *Playboy*, September 2004.
27   *Playboy*, September 2004.
28   *Playboy*, September 2004.
29   David Boyle, *Authenticity: Brands, fakes, spin and the lust for real life*, Flamingo, 2003.
30   David Boyle, *Authenticity: Brands, fakes, spin and the lust for real life*, Flamingo, 2003.

6. Inside Google

1   Google.com website, January 3, 2005.
2   *Playboy*, September 2004.
3   *Guardian*, August 20, 2004.
4   Associated Press, July 23, 2004.
5   *USA Today*, August 26, 2003.

7. Great brand or great product?

1 Google.com website, January 3, 2005.
2 *Financial Times*, March 30, 2004.

8. Google future

1 Google.com website, January 3, 2005.
2 Bloomberg, August 17, 2004.
3 BBC News online, November 11, 2004.

All Day I Dream About Sport

The story of the adidas brand

Conrad Brunner

ISBN 1-904879-12-8 | £7.99

In the black and white photos commemorating West Germany's win in the 1954 soccer World Cup, adidas founder Adi Dassler stands next to the team captain and coach, clutching the Jules Rimet Trophy to his chest.

In the 2004 European Championships, rank outsiders Greece surprised the world by winning. Like West Germany 50 years before, they all wore adidas.

In the intervening 50 years, adidas almost went under. Screaming matches, personality clashes, cultural friction, departmental rivalry, plummeting sales, mountains of unwanted inventory, financial despair, uncertainty – that was the company in the mid-80s.

Conrad Brunner charts the story of the sports shoe (and more) company through both its star endorsers – like Jesse Owens, Dick Fosbury, Stan Smith, David Beckham, and most unlikely of all, rappers Run-DMC – and its charismatic leaders, from founder Adi and his son Horst – the "Godfather of Sportsbiz" – through French fraudster Bernard Tapie to the current "savior of adidas" Robert Louis-Dreyfus.

Brand America

The mother of all brands

Simon Anholt and Jeremy Hildreth

ISBN 1-904879-02-0 | £7.99

America is more than just a country – it's the biggest brand the world has ever known. That's the argument of this provocative book.

Launched, managed and advertised like a global brand since the Declaration of Independence, America has deliberately marketed itself, its culture and its products with deft salesmanship and sheer hard-nosed determination. But this 200-year-long success story now seems to be under threat. Today, America is a brand in trouble.

Brand America shows how the most powerful brand in history grew to greatness, how close it has come to throwing it all away, and what might still be done to salvage it. This is a book for anyone interested in what the future holds for the world's sole remaining superpower.

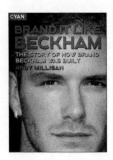

Brand It Like Beckham

The story of how Brand Beckham was built

Andy Milligan

ISBN 0-9542829-5-7 | £7.99

There is no one quite like David Beckham: brilliant footballer, dedicated athlete, fashion model, global icon and all-round celebrity, not to mention husband and father. But Beckham the brand? Well, yes. This book shows David Beckham in a new light: as a man who has harnessed his skills and his growing fame to market himself in the same professional and disciplined way that a successful company markets its brands.

Here is the story of a new breed of sportsman: one who is as comfortable with the trappings of marketing, fashion and the media as he is with team strips, playing surfaces and training grounds. By looking at the key choices David Beckham has made off the pitch, this book helps us understand how he has achieved his phenomenal commercial success. It provides fresh insights for readers who know about branding, a glimpse of a different side of Beckham for people who know about football, and an inspiring account of individual effort and achievement for all of us.

Great Ikea!

A brand for all the people

Elen Lewis

ISBN 1-904879-20-9 | £7.99

After you read this book, assembling flat pack furniture will never feel the same again!

Elen Lewis gives a witty and informative account of the ideas, principles, and history behind Ikea – a brand as well as a philosophy that has changed the way we furnish our homes, and made Swedish meatballs an essential part of the shopping experience. She explains how it arose from the vision of one man, Ingvar Kamprad, and how his belief that you change customer expectations rather than the product itself has created a worldwide icon.

Ikea has made stylish furniture affordable to everyone; but is it to our advantage that we now regard it as a disposable item? Where did those strange furnishing names come from? How come Ikea executives never stay at the Marriott? Why didn't Ikea furniture go down well at first in the United States? And is there really a secret route through the store for those who want to skip the kitchen and bathroom displays?

Both brand professionals and consumers can learn from this book. Take it with you when you next purchase a Billy bookcase.

Guinness is Guinness

*The colourful story of a
black and white brand*

Mark Griffiths

ISBN 1-904879-28-4 | £7.99

People say "Guinness is Guinness", but it's not as black and white as that. When you pick up that monochrome pint, you're about to taste 250 colourful years of global heritage whose ingredients are astounding innovation, obsessive quality, memorable advertising and a passionate devotion to remaining the world's top stout.

Guinness is Guinness tells the story of a truly global brand that's more than just a beer. Today, Guinness is accepted everywhere it trades because it employs local people, uses local resources, adapts to local tastes, advertises with local relevance and reverence as well as giving people a product they can enjoy and relax with. All are factors that combine to give a modern meaning to the 75-year old gone-but-not-forgotten advertising slogan, "Guinness is good for you." Does it really taste better in Ireland, its spiritual home? For those who want to get to the bottom of the glass, this book of stories reveals the answer to this and provides fascinating insights into a brand that has inspired warmth in drinkers and non-drinkers alike for a quarter of a millennium.

My Sister's a Barista

*How they made Starbucks
a home away from home*

John Simmons

ISBN 1-904879-27-6 | £7.99

Coffee is a commodity. You can get a cup at any café, sandwich bar or restaurant on any high street anywhere. So how did Starbucks manage to reinvent coffee as a whole new experience, and create a hugely successful brand in the process?

My Sister's a Barista tells the Starbucks story from its origins in a Seattle fish market to its growing global presence today. This is a story that has unfolded quickly – at least in terms of conventional business development. Starbucks is a phenomenon. Unknown 15 years ago, it now ranks among the 100 most valuable brands in the world. It employs 80,000 people in some 7,500 outlets from Bahrain to Beijing.

Starbucks is the quintessential brand of the modern age, built around the creation of an experience that can be consistently reproduced across the world. In exploring the secrets behind its success, this book also tackles the wider question of what makes a successful brand. This is a fascinating human story that will appeal to many different readers, and not just brand specialists.

Wizard!

Harry Potter's brand magic

Stephen Brown

ISBN 1-904879-30-6 | £7.99

Harry Potter is one of the most dazzling marketing triumphs of recent years. Less than a decade ago, the boy wizard's creator was living in abject poverty. Today, J. K. Rowling bestrides a $4 billion marketing empire. True, the Potter brand has not yet attained the instant recognition of Nike's swoosh, Coke's curlicues or McDonald's golden arches. But it's only a matter of time before Harry's lightning bolt ascends to the logosphere to occupy its rightful place in the marketing empyrean.

Wizard! tells the remarkable story of the Harry Potter brand. It is a story about stories: the story of the author, the books, the movies, the merchandise, the critics, the consumers – the story of the whole Harry Potter phenomenon, in fact. It also tells how these stories clash, blend, breed and occasionally cancel each other out. There are lessons here for every marketing executive, irrespective of sector or specialism: the importance of magic, mystery and imagination, the place of serendipity, the role of storytelling, the secret of secrecy and the need for intrigue, not ingratiation, when it comes to capturing customers.

Brand Potter epitomizes the contemporary marketing condition. It is the shape of things to come. It exists in an Entertainment Economy of fads, crazes, smash hits, next big things and selling telling tales – a world where brands can go from zero to hero (and back to zero again) in no time at all.

But does this mean that the Harry Potter phenomenon is about to implode? Ah, that would be telling . . .